THE WESTERN FRONTIER LIBRARY

CAMPAIGNING WITH CROOK

CAMPAIGNING WITH CROOK

CAPTAIN CHARLES KING, U.S.A.

WITH AN INTRODUCTION BY DON RUSSELL

University of Oklahoma Press : *Norman*

Library of Congress Catalog Card Number: 64-11332
New edition copyright © 1964 by the University of Oklahoma Press, Norman,
Publishing Division of the University.
Manufactured in the U.S.A. First printing, 1964;
second printing, 1967; third printing, 1983.

INTRODUCTION

by Don Russell

THE SLOPE, covered with tangled, low shrubbery, became steeper and steeper; near the top a vertical cliff of jagged rocks stretched east and west the length of Sunset Mountain. Up there, First Lieutenant Charles King was sure, were the Tonto Apaches he had trailed for five days since they had driven off a herd of cattle at Verde Reservation. The cattle had been recovered the previous evening after a running fight at Snow Lake, and the detail of men to guard the herd had reduced King's command to fifteen troopers from Companies "A" and "K," Fifth U.S. Cavalry, and a few Yuma Apache scouts, who seemed little inclined to tangle with the Tontos.

Second Lieutenant George O. Eaton had taken charge of the troopers at the edge of the timber, ready to come on at a signal, while King with Sergeant Bernard Taylor of Company "A" and the Yuma scouts attempted to root out the Tontos. The scouts moved timidly, and after a quarter-hour or so King lost patience with them and pushed ahead with the Sergeant. In another quarter of an hour he reached a ledge at the foot of the cliffs, but found nothing. He directed Sergeant Taylor to look for a path to the summit toward the right and was about to turn to the left for a similar search when a Tonto arrow whizzed past his head and struck quivering in a stunted oak. Almost immediately a second arrow, better aimed, tore through flesh and muscles at the outer corner of his left eye. He sprang for the edge of the shelf and crouched behind a rock just as two rifle shots were fired at him. He shouted for the Yumas to come on, but they turned tail at the sound of the guns and fled down the mountainside.

King had a carbine, and he looked for a chance to use it. The whiz of another arrow drew his eyes to the left, and despite blood streaming down his face, he was able to hit one of two Tontos he saw among the rocks. As he started to reload there came a rattle of scattered shots; his arm hung useless, for a bullet had shattered it at the shoulder. There was nothing left to do but run for it in the hope he could reach his men before the Tontos could reach him.

Holding his helpless arm in his left hand, he leaped from rock to rock, and had gone only a few yards when his foot slipped and he slid sprawling for eight or ten feet, cutting a jagged slash in his forehead. Blood poured over his eyes and blinded him; he staggered on a few steps, but fell again; groped for his revolver; found it gone, lost in one of his tumbles.

As he lay there helpless, he heard Sergeant Taylor calling him and made feeble response. In a moment the Sergeant found the wounded officer, swung him across his shoulder, and started bounding down the mountainside—King was a little fellow, barely reaching the army's required height, and in those days so thin and wiry that he had been chosen rider to represent the army two years before in a famous race at the Metairie Jockey Club in New Orleans.

Twice Taylor stopped, put down the officer, and sent shot after shot up the hill, at least once tumbling a tall Tonto off a rock and perhaps killing another. Then he moved on, the dangling arm giving King terrible torture. The Lieutenant implored, even ordered, the Sergeant to put him down and leave, but Taylor paid no heed.

At the first sound of shots Lieutenant Eaton had spread his troopers in a skirmish line and began scrambling up the mountainside to the rescue. Skillfully the young officer, only a year out of West Point, took charge of the fight, ignoring the demoralized Yuma scouts who came tearing through his lines. Just as Sergeant Taylor had given out after a three-hundred-yard dash carrying the wounded officer, the troops came in sight; and in a few more minutes the two officers were reunited. King, still conscious, urged Eaton to push on; and within ten minutes the Tontos were driven off and their dead and wounded collected.

Taylor got the Medal of Honor, Eaton was recommended for a brevet, and King got a compound fracture of the left arm above the elbow. "Under ordinary circumstances it was an injury that required the arm to be amputated," said Surgeon Warren Day, who reached the field four or five days later, "but I told him if he would do as I told him I would try and save the arm, and my instructions were to drink a gallon of whiskey a day and remain in my quarters. And he did both. I made a mule litter and we packed him from Sunset Pass to Camp Verde and took care of him there for about two months."

Thus the fight at Sunset Pass, Arizona Territory, on November 1, 1874, very nearly ended the career of Charles King two years before the Big Horn and Yellowstone Expedition against the Sioux, and six years before he was to write about it. Yet had not the Tonto's bullet shattered his right arm, it is improbable that Charles King would ever have written *Campaigning with Crook,* or any of the sixty or so books that came from his pen.

"From his pen" is a figure of speech, for he found handwriting very painful because of his injured arm. However, he had struggled through ten books by 1890, when he became the first author to produce books by the use of a dictating machine. He employed Miss Lucile Rhoades as "typewriter"—the operator was so called before the machine was—and an Ediphone as principals in what became known as a fiction factory. Appropriately the first novel she typed from a cylindrical record was titled *Sunset Pass*. Six more books were added to his bibliography that year. She continued in his employ for the rest of his life. They averaged better than two books a year through 1909.

Whether laboriously written by hand or dictated in a fiction factory, King's novels failed to achieve rank as great literature. They were much alike; one observer has noted that of fifty-one novels, all except seven rely upon wrongly assessed circumstantial evidence in their plot structure, and twenty-eight have one or more characters accused of wrongdoing on the same basis. A literary historian states flatly that King's novels were too hackneyed and sentimental to survive. Another notes: "Since the popular novel-reading public has become more sophisticated in its demands, King has disappeared from the novel to reappear on the TV screen and in the popular Western movie." While the screen has largely replaced the printed page for blood-and-thunder entertainment, one amendment is offered: King was never *that* hackneyed.

King's work was not literature, but it was not without merit, even literary merit. One does not condemn Remington because he is not Rembrandt or "Home on the Range" because it is not Beethoven's *Ninth Symphony*. Owen Wister, who was diemaker for the "Western" with his *The Virginian,* paid tribute to two predecessors, Mary Hallock Foote, "a voice lifted to honor the cattle country and not to libel it," and Charles King, who "opened for us the door upon frontier military life. . . . They (so far as I know) were the first that ever burst into that silent sea." King was not only the first, but also he was the most articulate of those who wrote of army life in Indian-fighting days. His romances were so realistic that a young lieutenant wrote (in 1896), "When we joined our regiments later at the remote frontier posts, we found there pretty nearly the things he had taught us to expect."

King's books were more than mere adventure stories; they were social documents. *"Laramie"; or, The Queen of Bedlam,* published in 1889, has a subtitle, "A Story of the Sioux War in 1876," yet no Indian fight is described in its pages, the entire action taking place at Fort Laramie, mainly in its bachelor officers' quarters called "Bedlam." As one commentator noted, King was not as "slaughterous" as either Dumas or Stevenson, but no writer of his time received more acclaim than King for vivid depiction of battle action. Lord Wolseley, commander in chief of the British army, called the description of the cavalry fight at Gettysburg in *Between the Lines* the best thing of the kind he had ever read.

More than half of all King's books were about the army of the frontier, including *The Colonel's Daughter,* first of his published novels and a perennial favorite, *Marion's Faith, Captain Blake, Foes in Ambush, An Army Wife,* and many more. Remington illustrated *A Daughter of the Sioux, An Apache Princess,* and *To the Front. A War-time Wooing, The General's Double, The Iron Brigade, The Rock of Chickamauga,* and five more were about the Civil War; and two more were about the Reconstruction period. *Found in the Philippines* and four more about the Philippine Insurrection gave King almost exclusive title to that subject. Several were juveniles, and many a boy swore by *Cadet Days,* a story of West Point, *Trumpeter Fred,* or *From School to Battlefield.*

His books appeared under sixty-nine different titles, not counting an autobiography called *Memories of a Busy Life* and a few other items not bound in cloth. Duplications of content reduce this by half a dozen, or, by taking advantage of all combination offers, you could have it all in fifty-seven volumes. There are also two hundred or more short stories, articles, introductions, and other contributions, of which half or more are uncollected.

That would seem enough to justify "a busy life," but King was also a soldier. On June 30, 1932, less than a year before his death on March 17, 1933, he was credited with seventy years of active service. It may be justifiably complained that as a fiction writer he lacked imagination, for his books reflected very closely events in his long military career.

Charles King was born on October 12, 1844, in Albany, New York, of a family of some distinction in American history. His father, Rufus King, a graduate of West Point, became a major general in the Civil War. His grandfather, another Charles King, was president of Columbia College —not yet a university—and two uncles, John Alsop King and James Gore King, were of sufficient importance to be included in the *Dictionary of American Biography.* The father of these three notables and great-grandfather of our Charles King was also a Rufus King, signer of the Constitution of the United States and last candidate of the Federalist party for President.

When Charles was one year old he was brought to Milwaukee, Wisconsin, where his father became editor of the *Milwaukee Sentinel* and achieved some prominence in politics and in militia. At the age of twelve, young Charles became a "marker" for the Milwaukee Light Guard—the duty of marker was to mark turning movements in the complicated close-order drill of that day.

At the beginning of the Civil War, Rufus King commanded a brigade—later famous as "The Iron Brigade"—in the defenses of Washington. Young Charles accompanied his father as mounted orderly, a volunteer position without pay. He witnessed the organization of the Army of the Potomac, but before it took the field, he received an appointment to West Point from President Lincoln.

In his senior year Charles King became cadet adjutant, the highest obtainable honor. Then came disaster. Even after one hundred years West Pointers are wary of naming names or releasing details of the academy's most notorious scandal. Cadet Orsemus B. Boyd was falsely accused of various petty thefts; and when marked bills were found in his room, he was paraded as a degraded criminal before the Battalion of Cadets at evening dress parade and drummed off the reservation, Cadet Adjutant King being in charge in the absence of all officers, as had not been uncommon in wartime. On his way out the disgraced cadet met Brevet Major General George W. Cullum, superintendent of the academy, who ordered an investigation. A board of inquiry found the evidence insufficient and advised trial by court-martial of five ringleaders in the affair. They pleaded guilty and were sentenced to be dismissed, but the sentences were suspended. King was deprived of his offices as cadet lieutenant and adjutant. Within a few months a younger cadet confessed the stealing, but it was several years before Boyd's classmates learned of his innocence. It was this affair that gave King his obsession with wrongly assessed circumstantial evidence.

King was graduated in 1866 and joined Light Battery "D" of the First Artillery in New Orleans that fall. For a time he commanded the Gatling gun platoon, several times called out to quell Reconstruction riots but never used, since rioting stopped when the rapid-fire guns appeared on the streets. In 1869 he went to Cincinnati on recruiting duty, and while there played with the Cincinnati Red Stockings, pioneer professional baseball team. His next assignment was as instructor at West Point.

Promoted to first lieutenant in 1870, he was transferred to the Fifth Cavalry. He served with his regiment at Fort McPherson, Nebraska, only long enough to become acquainted with its chief of scouts, Buffalo Bill, before its colonel, William H. Emory, ordered to district command in his brevet rank of major general, took King back to New Orleans as aide-de-camp. During that tour King was married to Miss Adelaide Lavender Yorke. In 1874 he joined Company "K" of his regiment at Camp Verde, Arizona Territory, and had fights with Apaches at Diamond Butte and Black Mesa before the one at Sunset Pass that took him out of service for a year.

King was acting regimental adjutant during the Sioux campaign in 1876, of which he tells in *Campaigning with Crook*. In 1877 he was acting assistant adjutant general for Brevet Major General Wesley Merritt during railway riots in Chicago and in the fall campaign against Chief Joseph and the Nez Percés. King was then adjutant of the Fifth Cavalry at Fort D. A. Russell, Wyoming Territory, until promoted captain in 1879 and retired because of continued trouble with the wound received at Sunset Pass.

In 1880 he became professor of military science and tactics at the University of Wisconsin. He also served as instructor of the state militia and was named successively colonel and aide-de-camp to the governor, acting inspector general, colonel commanding a regiment, and adjutant general of the state with the rank of brigadier general. At the beginning of the Spanish-American War he was commissioned brigadier general of volunteers. He was briefly first commanding general of the Department of Hawaii and commanded the First Brigade, First Division, Eighth Corps, in early battles of the Philippine Insurrection. Because of ill health he was discharged from the volunteer service on August 2, 1899, but was commissioned brigadier general in the Wisconsin National Guard in 1904 and promoted to major general in 1929. As National Guard instructor he served in his rank as captain, retired, until 1918, when he was advanced to major on the retired list, and in 1922 to lieutenant colonel. He also drilled cadets at the Michigan Military Academy, Orchard Lake, and at St. John's Military Academy, Delafield, Wisconsin, and served a term as member of the Board of Visitors to the United States Military Academy at West Point.

While all this was going on, it is to be recalled that the presses were rolling out those sixty-nine books signed "by Captain Charles King," and eventually "by General Charles King." The first of these is said to have started with the suggestion that Captain King as an army officer must be experienced in the sweetness of doing nothing. King rose to this challenge and told members of a downtown Milwaukee club what life in the army was like when Sioux and Cheyennes were on the warpath. He held them fascinated, and a member of the *Milwaukee Sentinel* staff who was present asked King to write it out as a Sunday feature. The result was Chapter IX of *Campaigning with Crook,* "The Fight of the Rear Guard." The local angle is still there with mention of the "Badger State Benefit"—Major Upham of Milwaukee in command, Lieutenant Bishop of Fond du Lac, Sergeant Goll, another home-town boy, and the Adjutant who had been "marker of our Light Guard" years before—King himself. Major Upham's final remark, "Eight o'clock here; church time in Milwaukee," and the concluding comment, "Who would have thought it was Sunday?" give it away as a Sunday supplement article.

The *Sentinel* asked for more as Buffalo Bill happened along on a tour of his theatrical combination and suggested a tribute to his friend Buffalo Chips White. That was the second article. Having written all around "The Combat at Slim Buttes," King found that subject appropriate for the third in the series. Other chapters followed in haphazard order. They were assembled without revision, despite which the book shows a few lapses of continuity. (There are two independent versions of "The Fight on the War Bonnet," where Buffalo Bill killed Yellow Hand, and some argument has been based on the lesser reference. King's detailed story holds up; for a discussion of the evidence see *The Lives and Legends of Buffalo Bill,* by Don Russell [University of Oklahoma Press, 1960], pages 214–35.)

The series was reprinted by the *Milwaukee Sentinel* in a paperback of perhaps five hundred copies as *Campaigning with Crook* with an over-title at top of the title page, *The Fifth Cavalry in the Sioux War of 1876.* The preface was dated May 25, 1880, and the small printing was sold out within a year, mainly to King's Wisconsin friends and participants in the campaign.

One new chapter was written for the pamphlet, appropriately called "Dropped Stitches." In it King again made unwarranted accusations on the basis of wrongly assessed circumstantial evidence—one would think he would have learned that lesson the first time.

In discussing the newspaper correspondents who accompanied the expedition, King said:

With one exception they proved excellent campaigners, and welcome, indeed, genial associates; but the exception was probably one of the most unhappy wretches on the face of the globe. He had come out as a novice the year previous, and had accompanied Colonel Dodge's exploring expedition to the Black Hills, and before long developed traits of character that made him somewhat of a nuisance. He was wofully green, a desperate coward, but so zealous in the cause of journalism that anything he fancied might interest the readers of the paper of which he announced himself "commissioner" was sent on irrespective of facts in the case. The officers found him taking notes of their conversations, jotting down everything he saw and heard around camp, caught him prying into matters that were in nature confidential, and so one night they terrified him to the verge of dissolution by preparations for defence and the announcement that the cooing and wooing of an army of wood-doves were the death chants of hundreds of squaws as the warriors were stripping for combat. Another time they primed him into writing a four-column despatch descriptive of the "Camelquo," a wonderful animal found only in the Black Hills, the offspring of the Rocky Mountain elk and the Egyptian camel, the latter being some of the animals introduced into Texas just before the war for transportation purposes, who had, so Mr. D. overheard, escaped from the rebels and made their way to the Northern plains during the great rebellion, and there had intermarried with the great elk, the native of the Hills. The resultant "Camelquo," so Mr. D. enthusiastically informed his paper, was an animal of the stature of the giraffe, the antlers of the elk, the humps of the camel, the fleetness and endurance of both parents, and the unconquerable ferocity of the tiger. How D. came to discover the sell in time, my informant Dr. McGillicuddy, did not remember, but to this day maps of the Black Hills bear commemoration of the incident, and Camelquo Creek is almost as well known as Spring and Rapid. Many a rough miner has asked since '75 how in Hades, or words to that effect, they came to have such queer names for their streams in the hills. Most of them were named by Colonel Dodge's party, and there was rhyme or reason in each, even for Amphibious Creek, which, said McGillicuddy, we so named because it sank out of sight so often and came up smiling so unexpectedly that it only seemed half land, half water.

On the campaign of '76, Mr. D—— again made his appearance as commissioner, started with General Crook's staff, but ere long was called upon to find new accommodations elsewhere. How it all came about I never cared to know, but after unpleasant experiences with first one set and then another, he gravitated eventually to the packers, who made him do guard and herd duty. He pushed ahead with Major Mills's command, and stumbled with them into the morning' battle at Slim Buttes. This he witnessed in a state of abject terror, and then, when the danger was over, wrote a most scandalous account, accusing Major Mills of all manner of misbehavior. His paper published it, but had to eat humble pie, make a most complete apology, and, I think, dismiss its correspondent. Camelquo Creek is the only existing trace of poor D—— of which we have any knowledge.

Eleven years after these lines were written Captain King found more than a trace of Reuben B. Davenport of the *New York Herald*. The unjustly accused reporter threatened suit for libel in October, 1890, and Harper and Brothers withdrew the book. King's investigations convinced him that the charges of cowardice were entirely false, and he replaced this entire passage with the apology that appeared on pages 153–55 of a new edition, still dated 1890 on the title page, and in subsequent printings without date on the title page. The rewritten passage is on pages 144–46 of the present edition.

For another correspondent, John F. Finerty of the *Chicago Times,* King had only praise. Finerty's *War-Path and Bivouac* was published in 1890, the same year as the reprinting of *Campaigning with Crook.* They were followed in 1891 by *On the Border with Crook,* by Captain John G. Bourke of General Crook's staff. Few Indian campaigns were described by so many participants who were able writers. Among them there is no major disagreement, yet each contributes an individual point of view. King's unique contribution is the story of the campaign of the Fifth Cavalry prior to its joining the Crook expedition.

Many recent writers on the Custer disaster have assumed the plan of campaign to have been a converging of the commands of Crook, Gibbon, and Terry against the Sioux on the Little Big Horn, and that this plan failed when Crook withdrew after his fight on the Rosebud a week before the defeat of Custer's Seventh Cavalry, detached from Terry's column. Sheridan's orders show clearly that no such plan was contemplated. That as many as five thousand to nine thousand Indians would be found in one village was unprecedented; it was supposed rather that they would be scattered in small bands, with five hundred to eight hundred warriors the most to be expected in any one place. The objective was to contain these bands within an area that might be described as Wyoming north of the Platte and Montana south of the Yellowstone, and to round them up, if possible.

The Fifth Cavalry, with eight of its twelve companies present (two more joined later) was assigned to scout between the columns of Crook and Terry, mainly along the Mini Pusa, or South Cheyenne River, southwest of the Black Hills. The Fifth was ordered to join Crook after his withdrawal from the Rosebud, but delayed to turn back a band of Cheyennes bolting from Red Cloud Agency. In the resulting encounter the regiment's chief of scouts, Mr. William F. Cody, was conspicuous; so says the regimental history. But this story and many another are well told by Captain Charles King, with no need for further explanation or amplification.

PREFACE

by Captain Charles King, U.S.A.

TEN YEARS AGO, at the request of the editor of a paper at my old home, these sketches of the Sioux Campaign of 1876 were written and, finding favor with comrades to whom a few were sent, were published in pamphlet form. Now, reinforced by certain other sketches which have since appeared, they are given a new framework.

They were the first fruits, so to speak, of a pen that has since been seldom idle. They were rough sketches, to be sure, but no rougher than the campaign; and in the early days of a divorce from associations that were very dear, and of a return to surroundings once familiar, yet, after twenty years of absence, so changed that a cat in a strange garret could hardly have felt less at home, I laid their faint tribute of respect and honor at the feet of the soldier who had been our commander in the wild days in Arizona, our leader from the Platte to the Yellowstone, and our comrade in every hardship and privation—Brigadier-General George Crook, United States Army.

Only enough of these pamphlets were printed to reach the few hundred comrades who rode the grim circuit of "The Bad Lands" in that eventful centennial year. The little edition was long ago exhausted. The years that followed only served to strengthen the ties that bound me to the revered commander of old cavalry days. Many a name recorded in these pages no longer graces our muster rolls. Mason, our soldier major, gallant Emmet Crawford, brave old Munson, daring Philo Clark; Rodgers and Price, Egan and Dewees, Bache and Hunter, have been called from the ranks in which they won such honor; and, only a few short months ago, the leader whom they so faithfully served rejoined them on the farther shore of the dark and silent river. The mountains and prairies over which we marched and fought know no longer the war cry of painted savages or the din of thrilling combat. Herds of browsing cattle crowd the lovely valleys through which we drove the buffalo. Peaceful homes and smiling villages dot the broad Northwest where hardly a roof tree was in place when Crook essayed the task of subjugating the foeman to settlement and civilization. Another star had been added to the one awarded him for the campaign which left the fierce Apaches conquered and disarmed. The highest grade in the army had been attained when, all too soon, he was summoned to answer to his name, "beyond the veil."

Better pens than mine shall tell our people of his long years of brave and faithful service in which this campaign of '76—so pregnant with interest to us who rode the trail, and with result to a waiting nation—was, after all, only an episode; but, just as in honor and in loyalty, these faint pictures of the stirring scenes through which he led us were inscribed to him at their birth, so now, with added honor and in affectionate remembrance tenfold increased, is that humble tribute renewed.

CHARLES KING,
Captain, U.S.A.

CONTENTS

ILLUSTRATIONS

MAP

CAMPAIGNING WITH CROOK

ONE

FORT HAYS AND THE START

THE DISASTROUS BATTLE on the Little Horn, which resulted in the annihilation of General Custer and his five favorite companies of the Seventh Cavalry, occurred on the 25th of June, 1876. On the 4th of that month, we of the Fifth Cavalry were far to the south, scattered over the boundless prairies of Kansas. Regimental headquarters and four companies occupied the cosey quarters of Fort Hays, nearly midway between Leavenworth and Denver, Missouri and the mountains, and Company "K," of which I then was first lieutenant, had pitched its tents along the banks of a winding fork of the Smoky Hill River, wondering why we had been "routed out" from our snug barracks and stables at Fort Riley, and ordered to proceed, "equipped for field service," to Hays City by rail. Ordinarily, Uncle Sam pays the costly railway fare for horsemen and their steeds only when danger is imminent. The two posts were but a week's easy march apart; not a hostile Indian had been seen or heard of in all Kansas since the previous winter; General Pope, who commanded the department, had won the hearts of the ladies and children of the officers' families by predicting that there would be no separation from husbands and fathers that summer at least; all the ladies had "joined," and, after our long sojourn in the wilds of Arizona, where but few among them had been able to follow us, we were rejoicing in their presence and luxuriating in the pretty homes ornamented and blessed by their dainty handiwork. Some among their number had never before appeared in garrison, and were taking their first lesson in frontier experience. Some, too, had only been with us six short weeks, and did not dream that the daily parades in which they took so much delight, the sweet music of our band, the brilliant uniforms and dancing plumes that lent such color and life to rapid drill or stately guard mounting, were one and all but part and parcel of the preparation for scenes more stirring, far less welcome to such gentle eyes.

Fort Hays was joyous with mirth and music and merry laughter, for some of the ladies of the regiment had brought with them from the distant East younger sisters or friends, to whom army life on the plains was a revelation, and in whose honor a large barrack-room had been transformed into "the loveliest place in the world for a german," and Strauss's sweetest music rose and fell in witching invitation after the evening tattoo. Riding, driving, and hunting parties were of daily occurrence, and more than one young fellow's heart seemed in desperate jeopardy when the summons came.

The sun was setting in a cloudless sky as I reined in my horse in front of General Carr's quarters and dismounted to make my report of a three day's hunt along the valley of the Saline for stampeded horses. The band, in their neat summer dress, were grouped around the flagstaff, while the strains of "Soldaten Lieder" thrilled through the soft evening air, and, fairly carried away by the cadence of the sweet music, a party of young ladies and officers had dropped their croquet mallets and were waltzing upon the green carpet of the parade. Seated upon the verandas, other ladies and older officers were smilingly watching the pretty scene,

4

and on the western side of the quadrangle the men in their white stable frocks were just breaking ranks after marching up from the never-neglected care of their horses. Half a dozen laughing children were chasing one another in noisy glee, their bright sashes and dainty dresses gleaming in the last rays of the golden orb. The General himself was gazing thoughtfully at the distant line of willows that fringed the banks of the stream, and holding an open newspaper in his hand as I entered and made my report.

"Have you heard the news?" he asked me. "Schuyler has gone to join General Crook as aide-de-camp. Got a telegram from him just after you left on this scout, and started last night. It's my belief that Crook will have a big campaign, and that we'll be sent for."

Ten minutes after, as the trumpets rang out the "retreat," and the last echoes of the evening gun died away over the rolling prairie, we noted a horseman coming at rapid gait along the dusty road from Hays City, as the railway station was hopefully named. He disappeared among the foliage in the creek bottom. The soft hush of twilight fell upon the garrison, the band had gone away to supper, the bevy of sweet-faced girls with their tireless escorts had gathered with a number of officers and ladies in front of the General's quarters, where he and I were still in conversation, when the horseman, a messenger from the telegraph office, re-appeared in our midst. "Despatch for you, General; thought you'd better have it at once," was all he said, as he handed it to "the chief," and, remounting, cantered away.

Carr opened the ugly brown envelope and took out, not one, but three sheets of despatch paper, closely written, and began to read. Looking around upon the assembled party, I noticed that conversation had ceased and a dozen pair of eyes were eagerly scrutinizing the face of the commanding officer. Anxious hearts were beating among those young wives and mothers, and the sweet girl faces had paled a little in sympathy with the dread that shone all too plainly in the eyes of those who but so recently had undergone long and painful separation from soldier husbands. The General is a sphinx; he gives no sign. Slowly and carefully he reads the three pages; then goes back and begins over again. At last, slowly, thoughtfully he folds it, replaces the fateful despatch in its envelope, and looks up expectant of question. His officers, restrained by discipline, endeavor to appear unconcerned, and saying nothing. The ladies, either from dread of the tidings of awe of him, *look* volumes, but are silent. Human nature asserts itself, however, and the man and the commander turns to me with, "Well, what did I tell you?" And so we got our orders for the Sioux campaign of 1876.

To the officers, of course, it was an old story. There was not one of our number who had not seen hard campaigning and sharp Indian fighting before. But could we have had our choice, we would have preferred some less abrupt announcement. Hardly a word was spoken as the group broke up and the ladies sought their respective homes, but the bowed heads and hidden faces of many betrayed the force of the blow.

The officers remained with General Carr to receive his instructions. There was no time to lose, and the note of preparation sounded on the spot. General Sheridan's orders directed four companies from Fort Hays to proceed at once to Cheyenne by rail, and there await the coming of the more distant companies—eight in all, to go on this, the first alarm.

Companies "A," "B," "D," and "K" were designated to go; "E" to stay and "take care of the shop." Those to go

6

were commanded by married officers, each of whom had to leave wife and family in garrison. "E" had a bachelor captain, and a lieutenant whose better half was away in the East, so the ladies of the regiment were ready to mob the General for his selection; but there was wisdom in it. In ten minutes the news was all over the post. A wild Celtic "Hurray, fellows, we're going for to join Crook," was heard in the barracks, answered by shouts of approval and delight from every Paddy in the command. Ours is a mixed array of nationalities—Mulligan and Meiswinkel, Crapaud and John Bull, stand shoulder to shoulder with Yanks from every portion of the country. In four regiments only is exclusiveness as to race permitted by law. Only darkies can join their ranks. Otherwise, there is a promiscuous arrangement which, oddly enough, has many a recommendation. They balance one another as it were—the phlegmatic Teuton and the fiery Celt, mercurial Gaul and stolid Anglo-Saxon. Dashed and strongly tinctured with the clearheaded individuality of the American, they make up a company which for *personnel* is admirably adapted to the wants of our democratic service. The company of the Fifth Cavalry most strongly flavored with Irish element in the ranks was commanded by Captain Emil Adam, an old German soldier, whose broken English on drill was the delight of his men. "The representative Paddy," as he calls himself, Captain Nick Nolan, of the Tenth Cavalry, has an Ethiopian lieutenant (a West Pointer) and sixty of the very best darkies that ever stole chickens. But wherever you meet them, the first to hurray at the chance of a fight is the Pat, and no matter how gloomy or dismal the campaign, if there be any fun to be extracted from its incidents, he is the man to find it.

And so our Irishmen gave vent to their joy, and with

7

whistling and singing the men stowed away their helmets and full-dress uniforms, their handsome belts and equipments, and lovingly reproduced the old Arizona slouch hats and "thimble belts," and the next evening our Fort Hays command, in two special trains, was speeding westward as fast as the Kansas Pacific could carry us. The snow-capped peaks of the Rockies hove in sight next day, and Denver turned out in full force to see us go through. At evening on the 7th, we were camping on the broad prairie near Cheyenne. Here Major Upham joined us with Company "I." A week after we were off for Laramie. On the 22d, our companies were ordered straight to the north to find the crossing of the broad Indian trail from the Red Cloud and Spotted Tail reservations, by which hundreds of Indians were known to be going to the support of Sitting Bull and Crazy Horse.

We were to hide in the valley of the South Cheyenne, near the base of the Black Hills, and cut off the Indian supplies. Buffalo Bill had joined us, his old comrades of the Sioux war of 1868–69; and though we feared the Indians would be quick to detect our presence and select others of a dozen routes to the Powder River country, we hoped to be able to nab a few.

On the 24th, we had begun our march at 6 A.M. from the Cardinal's Chair, at the head of the Niobrara, and before noon had descended into the valley of "Old Woman's Fork," of the South Cheyenne. We had with us two half-breed Sioux scouts and an Indian boy, "Little Bat," who had long been employed by the Fort Laramie officers as a reliable guide. Camping at noon along the stream, I was approached by Major Stanton, who had joined our column under instructions from General Sheridan, and informed that he was going to push ahead of the column at once, as the scouts reported recent Indian signs. It was necessary, he said, that

8

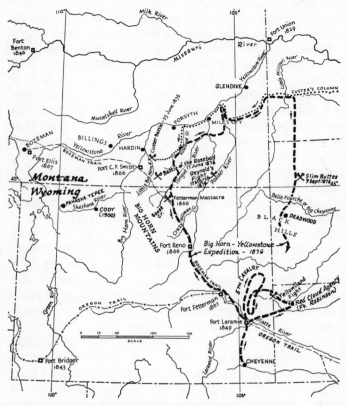

From Don Russell's *The Lives and Legends of Buffalo Bill* (Norman, 1960)

Routes of Fifth Cavalry and Big Horn and Yellowstone Expedition in the Sioux War of 1876

he should get to the Cheyenne as quickly as possible, and he wanted me to go as commander of the escort. In half an hour we were in saddle again, Major Stanton with his blunderbuss of a rifle, "Little Bat" in his semi-civilized garb, Lieutenant Keyes with forty men of Company "C," and myself. The General detained me a moment to convey some earnest instructions, and to post me on certain points in Sioux warfare which experience with Apaches was supposed to have dulled, and, with the promise, "I'll follow on your trail tomorrow," waved his hand, and in two minutes we were out of sight down the winding valley.

Three P.M. is early on a long June day. We rode swiftly, steadily, but cautiously northward; the valley widened out to east and west; we made numerous cutoffs among the bends of the stream, crossing low ridges, at each one of which Bat, well to the front, would creep to the top, keenly scrutinize all the country around, and signal "come on." At 5 o'clock he suddenly halted and threw himself from his horse, and I cantered forward to see what was up. We had struck our first trail of the campaign, and the yielding soil was thick with pony tracks. Coming from the east, the direction of the reservation, they led straight down the valley, and we followed. Every now and then other tracks from the east joined those we were on, and though at least four or five days old, they were of interest. Half an hour before sunset, far off among the hills to the northeast, a thin column of smoke shot up into the clear sky. Ten minutes more another rose in the west. They were Sioux signals, and we were discovered. But the country was open all around us; not a tree except the cottonwoods along the narrow stream-bed, no fear of ambuscade, and we must not halt until within sight of the Cheyenne Valley; so on we go. Just at twilight, Bat, five hundred yards in front, circles his horse

10

rapidly to the left, and again I join him. It is the recent
trail of a war party of Sioux, crossing the valley, and disappearing among the low hills to the northwest. They number fifty warriors, and those whose tracks we have been following took the same direction—the short cut towards the
Big Horn mountains. Our march is very cautious now—
advance, flankers, and rear guard of old, tried soldiers, well
out; but on we jog through the gathering darkness, and at
nine P.M., as we ride over a ridge, Bat points out to me a
long, low line of deeper shade winding six or seven miles
away in the moonlight. It is the timber along the Cheyenne,
and now we may hunt for water and give our tired horses
rest and grass. The valley is broad; the water lies only in
scanty pools among the rocks in the stream bed. There has
been no rain for a month, and there is not a blade of
grass neared than the bluffs, a mile away. Our horses drink
eagerly, and then in silence we fill our canteens and move
off towards the hills. Here I find a basin about two hundred
yards in diameter in which we "half lariat" and hobble our
horses, dig holes in the ground, wherein, with sagebrush
for fuel, we build little fires and boil our coffee, while Keyes
and I take a dozen of our men and post them around our
bivouac at points commanding every approach. No Indian
can reach us unseen through that moonlight. No Indian
cares to attack at night, unless he has a "sure thing"; and
though from five different points we catch the blaze of
signal fires, we defy surprise, and with ready carbine by our
side we eat our crisp bacon, sip the welcome tin of steaming
coffee, then light our pipes and chat softly in the cool night
air. Little we dream that two hundred miles away Custer
is making his night ride to death. Our supports are only
twenty-five miles away. We dread no attack in such force
that we cannot "stand off" until Carr can reach us, and, as

I make my rounds among the sentinels to see that all are vigilant, the words of the Light Cavalryman's song are sounding in my ears:

> *The ring of a bridle, the stamp of a hoof,*
> *Stars above and the wind in the tree;*
> *A bush for a billet, a rock for a roof,*
> *Outpost duty's the duty for me.*
> *Listen! A stir in the valley below—*
> *The valley below is with riflemen crammed,*
> *Cov'ring the column and watching the foe;*
> *Trumpet-Major! Sound and be d——.*

Bang! There's a shot from below, and the bivouac springs to life.

TWO

THE TRAIL AND THE CHASE

A SHOT in the dead of night from an outpost in the heart of the Indian country is something that soon ceases to be either exciting or of great interest, but the first that is heard on the campaign makes the pulses bound. Men sprang to their feet, horses pawed and snorted, and the sergeant of the guard and myself made rapid time to the point from which the alarm had come. There was the sentinel alone, unharmed, but perturbed in spirit. To the question, somewhat sternly put, "Who fired that shot?" he replies, with evident chagrin, "I did, sir; somethin' was crawlin' right up that holler, an' I challenged an' he didn't answer, an' I fired; but danged if I know what it was." Before there is time to say a word of rebuke, plainly enough in the bright moonlight something *does* come crawling up out of a "hollow" two hundred yards away—something of a yellow or reddish brown, on four legs, with a long, smooth, sneaking shamble that carries the quadruped rapidly over the ground, then changes to an ungainly lope, which takes him to a safe distance in six seconds; and there the creature turns, squats on his haunches, and coolly surveys us. Turning away in silent indignation, as I get almost out of earshot it is some comfort to hear the sergeant's pithy commentary, "Ye wall-eyed guttersnipe, your grandmother would ha' known that was nothin' but a coyote."

Then follows the inevitable volley of chaff with which the Paddy greets every blunder on the part of his fellow soldiers, and for a few minutes the silent bivouac is rollicking with fun. That some recent attempt has been made to instruct the troopers of Company "C" in the finesse of sentry duty is apparent from the shouted query, "Hi, Sullivan, if it was *two* cayotes would you advance the saynior or the junior wid the countersign?" at which there is a roar, and Lieutenant Keyes visibly blushes. In half an hour all is quiet again. Officers and men, we watch turn and turn about during the night, undisturbed, save at 3 o'clock the outlying sentries report that they distinctly heard the rapid beat of many hoofs dying away towards the west.

We are astir at the first gray of dawn, rolling our blankets and promptly saddling; for we must ride well down the Cheyenne and find the Mini Pusa, the dry north fork, before breakfast can be attended to. No stirring trumpet marks our reveille. We mount in silence, and like shadowy spectres ride away northward in the broadening valley. The stars are not yet paling in the west, but Bat's quick eye detects fresh hoofprints not two hours old in the springy soil of the hillside, half a mile out from camp. Sure enough. They had prowled around us during the night, longing for our scalps, but not daring to attack. Only a few venturesome spies had galloped down to take observations and had then ridden away to join their brothers in arms and plot our destruction. We laughed as we shook our bridle reins and jogged along, thinking how confounded they would be when they caught sight of our main body, who, with General Carr at their head, would be along by noon. A six-mile ride brought us into the belt of cottonwoods and willows along the bed of the stream, but the South Cheyenne had sunk out of sight. Broad reaches of streaked and rippled sand wound through the timber, clearly showing where, earlier in the season, a rapid, sweeping torrent had borne great logs and heaps of brushwood upon its tawny breast; but it had dwindled away to nothing, and our thirsty horses looked reproachfully at their masters as, dismounting, we ploughed up the yielding sand in hopes of finding the needed water beneath. This is one of the dismal peculiarities of the streams of the Far West. On the 1st of May we would have found that valley barely fordable; on the 25th of June it was as dry as a bone.

Mounting again, and scattering through the timber "downstream," a shout from Major Stanton had the effect of the trumpet rally on skirmish drill.

Our party came together with eager haste and found him under a steep bank, shaded by willows, his horse fetlock deep in what remained of a once deep pool; and two or three at a time our chargers slaked their thirst. It was poor water —warm, soapy, alkaline—but better than none at all.

Just before noon we were clambering up the hills on the northeast of the Mini Pusa. Our orders were to proceed with the utmost caution on nearing the trail. General Sheridan had clearly indicated that it must cross the valley of the South Cheyenne some distance west of the Beaver, and very near its confluence with the Mini Pusa. Stanton and I with our field glasses in hand were toiling up through the yielding, sandy soil with Little Bat; Lieutenant Keyes and the escort, leading their horses, following. Once at the top of the ridge we felt sure of seeing the country to the eastward, and hardly had Bat reached the crest and peered cautiously over than he made a quick gesture which called the Major and myself to his side. He pointed to the southeast, and sweeping our glasses in that direction, we plainly saw the broad, beaten track. It looked like a great highway, deserted and silent; and it led from the thick timber in the Cheyenne Valley straight to the southeast up the distant slope and disappeared over the dim, misty range of hills in the direction of the Red Cloud and Spotted Tail reservations.

General Sheridan was right. Sitting in his distant office in Chicago, he was so thoroughly informed that he could order out his cavalry to search through a region hitherto known only to the Sioux and tell them just where they would find the highway by which the vast hordes of hostiles under Sitting Bull were receiving daily reinforcements and welcome supplies of ammunition from the agencies three and four hundred miles to the southeast.

This was the traffic which General Carr and the Fifth Cavalry were ordered to break up; and here, just at noon, our little band of three officers and forty men, far in the advance, had struck the trail, as General Sheridan predicted. Keeping horses and men well under cover, we crept to a farther ridge, and from there our glasses commanded a grand sweep of country: the valley of the South Cheyenne for fifty miles to the southeastward, until the stream itself was lost in the tortuous cañon of the Southern Black Hills; themselves forty miles to the eastward, and the lone peak far to the northeast that the Sioux called (phonetically spelling) Heengha Kahga. The earliest maps simplified that into "Inyan Kara," and now the school children of Deadwood talk glibly of the big hill that, higher than Harney's or Custer's Peak, their geography terms the "Indian Carry." Why can't we keep the original names?

Once thoroughly satisfied of our proximity to the trail, Major Stanton directed the escort to retrace its steps to the thick timber along the Mini Pusa, where it would be out of sight, while he and I, with our powerful binoculars, kept watch upon the Indian highway. The afternoon was hot and cloudless; not a breath of air stirred the clumps of sagebush, the only vegetation along the bluffs and slopes. The atmosphere was dazzling clear, and objects were visible to us through our glasses that we knew to be miles away. The signal smokes to the west, and our front of the day before, had disappeared; not a living thing was in sight. Our men and horses were hidden among the dense cottonwoods a mile behind us; but, though invisible to us, we well knew that trusty eyes were keeping watch for the first signal from the hillside.

Three—four o'clock came, and not a soul had appeared upon the Indian trail. Away over the intervening ridge to the rear we could see the valley of Old Woman's Fork, down which we had come the day previous, and our glasses detected, by an hour after noon, clouds of dust rising high in air, harbingers of the march of General Carr and the main body. At last the Major closed his glasses with a disgusted snap and the remark, "I don't believe there's an Indian stirring today."

Not in our sight—not within our hearing, perhaps. The blessed Sabbath stillness falls on all within our ken; our steeds are blinking, our men are drowsing in the leafy shades below. Only the rising dust, miles to the southward, reveals the coming of comrade soldiery. Far to the northwest, a single dark speck, floating against the blue of heaven, attracts the lingering inspection of my field glass. Eagle or buzzard, I do not know. The slow, circling, stately flight in ascending spiral carries him beyond our vision, but from his altitude the snow-capped peaks of the Big Horn range are clearly visible, and on this still Sabbath afternoon those mighty peaks are looking down upon a scene of carnage, strife, and slaughter that, a week hence, told only by curt official despatches, will thrill a continent with horror. Even

17

as we watch there on the slopes by the Mini Pusa, Stanton and I, grumbling at our want of luck in not sighting an Indian, many a true and trusted comrade, many an old cadet friend of boyish days, many a stalwart soldier is biting the dust along the Little Horn, and the names of Custer and his men are dropping from the muster rolls. The heroes of a still mightier struggle, the victors of an immortal defence of national honor, are falling fast till all are gone, victims of a thankless warfare.

No wonder the Indians have no time to bother with us. We bivouac in undisturbed serenity that night, and join our regiment in the Cheyenne Valley at noon next day without so much as an adventure. That night Company "I" is thrown forward to scout the trail while the regiment camps out of sight among the cottonwoods; and for the next week we keenly watch the neighborhood, all the companies making thorough scouts in each direction, but finding nothing of consequence. Small parties of Indians are chased, but easily escape, and there isn't a doubt that the reservation Indians know of our whereabouts, and so avoid us.

Late in the afternoon of July 1st, our new colonel, Wesley Merritt, famous as a cavalry commander during the War of the Rebellion, arrives and assumes the reins of government, relieving General Carr, who falls back to second in command. We are all agog to see what will be our new chief's first move. He is fresh from Sheridan's staff in Chicago, and is doubtless primed with latest instructions and wishes of the Lieutenant General. He is no stranger to us, nor we to him; and his first move is characteristic. At dawn of day of the 2d, he marches us four miles downstream to better grass and a point nearer the big trail; sends Montgomery with his grays to scout over towards the Black Hills,

18

and Hayes and Bishop with Company "G" to lie along the trail itself—but no Indian is sighted.

The sun is just rising on the morning of the 3d of July when my captain, Mason, and I roll out of our blankets and set about the very simple operations of a soldier's campaign toilet. The men are grooming their horses; the tap of the currycomb and the impatient pawing of hoofs is music in the clear, crisp, bracing air. Our cook is just announcing breakfast, and I am eagerly sniffing the aroma of coffee when General Merritt's orderly comes running through the trees. "Colonel Mason, the General directs Company "K" to get out as quickly as possible—Indians coming up the valley!" "Saddle up, men! Lively now!" is the order. We jump into boots and spurs, whip the saddles from saplings and stumps, rattle the bits between the teeth of our excited horses, sling carbines over shoulder, poke fresh cartridges into revolver chambers, look well to the broad horsehair "cinches," or girths. The men lead into line, count fours, mount, and then, without a moment's pause, "Fours right, trot," is the order, and Mason and I lead off at a spanking gait, winding through the timber and suddenly shooting out upon the broad, sandy surface of the dry stream bed. There the first man we see is Buffalo Bill, who swings his hat. "This way, Colonel, this way," and away we go on his tracks. "K" is a veteran company. Its soldiers are, with few exceptions, on their second and third enlistments. Its captain ranks all the line officers of the regiment, and admirably commanded it during the war while the field officers were doing duty as generals of volunteers. There is hardly a trace of nervousness even among the newest comers; but this is the first chase of the campaign for us, and all are eager and excited. Horses in rear struggle to rush to the front, and as we sputter out of the sand and strike the grassy slopes beyond the timber belt all break into a lope. Two or three scouts on a ridge five hundred yards ahead are frantically signalling to us; and, bending to the left again, we sweep around towards them, now at a gallop. Mason sternly cautions some of the eager men who are pressing close behind us, and, looking back, I see Sergeant Stauffer's bronzed face lighting up with a grin I used to mark in the old Apache campaigns in Arizona; and the veteran "Kelly" riding, as usual, all over his horse, but desperately bent on being ahead when we reach the scene. Left hands firmly grasp the already foaming reins, while throughout the column carbines are "advanced" in the other.

"Here comes Company 'I,' fellers," is the muttered announcement from the left and rear, and, glancing over my left shoulder, I see Kellogg with his bays and Lieutenant Reilly swinging out along the slope to our left. As we near the ridge and prepare to deploy, excitement is subdued but intense—Buffalo Bill, plunging along beside us on a strawberry roan sixteen hands high, gets a trifle of a lead; but we go tearing up the crest in a compact body, reach it, rein up, amazed and disgusted—not an Indian to be seen for two miles across the intervening "swale." Away to the left, towards the Cheyenne, scouts are again excitedly beckoning, and we move rapidly towards them; but slower now, for Mason will not abuse his horses for a wild-goose chase. Ten minutes bring us thither. Kellogg has joined forces with us, and the two companies are trotting in parallel columns. Still no Indian; but the scouts are ahead down the valley, and we follow for a brisk half-hour and find ourselves plunging through the timber ten miles east of camp. Another hour and we are dashing along a high ridge parallel with the Black Hills; and there, sure enough, are Indians, miles

20

ahead and streaking it for the Powder River country as fast as their ponies can carry them. We have galloped thirty miles in a big circle before catching sight of our chase, and our horses are panting and wearied. Every now and then we pass packsaddles with fresh agency provisions, which they had dropped in their haste. Once our scouts get near enough to exchange a shot or two; but at last they fairly beat us out of sight, and we head for home, reach camp, disgusted and empty-handed, about four P.M. Two "heavy-weights" (Colonel Leib's and Lieutenant Reilly's horses) drop dead under them, and the first pursuit of the Fifth is over.

THREE

THE FIGHT ON THE WAR BONNET

THE CHASE of July 3d, besides killing two and using up a dozen horses, rendered our further presence in the valley of the Cheyenne clearly useless. No more Indians would be apt to come that way when they had the undisturbed choice of several others. General Merritt was prompt to accept the situation and as prompt to act. Early the next morning, "K" and "I," the two companies engaged in the dash of the day before, took the direct back track up the valley of Old Woman's Fork, guarding the chief and the wagons. General Carr, with companies "B," "G," and "M," marched eastward towards the Black Hills, while Major Upham, with "A," "C," and "D," struck out northwestward up the valley of the Mini Pusa. Both commands were ordered to make a wide *detour*, scout the country for forty-eight hours, and rejoin headquarters at the head of what was then called Sage Creek. We of the centre column spent the glorious Fourth in a dusty march, and followed it up on the 5th with another.

On the 6th, a courier was sent in to Fort Laramie, seventy miles away, while the regiment camped along the stream to wait for orders. Towards ten o'clock on the following morning, while the camp was principally occupied in fighting flies, a party of the junior officers were returning from a refreshing bath in a deep pool of the stream, when

22

Buffalo Bill came hurriedly towards them from the General's tent. His handsome face wore a look of deep trouble, and he brought us to a halt in stunned, awe-stricken silence with the announcement, "Custer and five companies of the Seventh wiped out of existence. It's no rumor—General Merritt's got the official despatch."

Now we knew that before another fortnight the Fifth would be sent to reinforce General Crook on the Big Horn. Any doubts as to whether a big campaign was imminent was dispelled. Few words were spoken—the camp was stilled in soldierly mourning. That night Lieutenant Hall rode in with later news and letters. He had made the perilous trip from Laramie alone, but confirmed the general impression that we would be speedily ordered in to the line of the North Platte, to march by way of Fetterman to Crook's support. On Wednesday, the 12th, our move began, no orders having been received until the night before. Just what we were to do, probably no one knew but Merritt; he didn't tell, and I never asked questions. Evening found us camping near the Cardinal's Chair at the head of the Niobrara in a furious storm of thunder, lightning, and rain, which lasted all night, and, wet to the skin, we were glad enough to march off at daybreak on the 13th, and still more glad to camp again that evening under the lee of friendly old Rawhide Peak.

We were now just one long day's march from Fort Laramie, and confidently expected to make it on the following day. At reveille on the 14th, however, a rumor ran through the camp that Merritt had received despatches during the night indicating that there was a grand outbreak among the Indians at the reservation. Of course we knew that they would be vastly excited and encouraged by the intelligence of the Custer massacre. Furthermore, it was well known that there were nearly a thousand of the Cheyennes, the finest warriors and horsemen of the plains, who as yet remained peaceably at the Red Cloud or Spotted Tail Reservations alone the White River, but they were eager for a pretext on which to "jump," and now they might be expected to leave in a body at any moment and take to the warpath. Our withdrawal from the Cheyenne River left the favorite route again open; and the road to the Black Hills was again traversed by trains of wagons and large parties of whites on their way to the mines, a sight too tempting for their covetous eyes. Major Jordan, commanding the post of Camp Robinson, had hurriedly described the situation in a despatch to Merritt, and when "boots and saddles" sounded, and we rode into line; we saw the quartermaster guiding his wagons back over the ridge we had crossed the day before, and in a few minutes were following in their tracks. Away to the east we marched that morning, and at noon were halted where the road connecting Fort Laramie with the reservation crossed the Rawhide Creek. Here Captain Adam with Company "C" left us and pushed forward to the Niobrara Crossing, twenty-five miles nearer the Indian villages, while the indefatigable Major Stanton, "our polemical paymaster," was hurried off to Red Cloud, to look into the situation. The rest of us waited further developments.

On Saturday, the 15th of July, just at noon, General Merritt received the despatch from the Red Cloud Agency which decided the subsequent movement of his command. It led to his first "lightning march" with his new regiment; it impelled him to a move at once bold and brilliant. It brought about an utter rout and discomfiture among the would-be allies of Sitting Bull, and, while it won him the commendation of the Lieutenant General, it delayed us a week in finally reaching Crook, and there was some implied criticism in remarks afterwards made.

The Fight on the War Bonnet

In a mere narrative article there is little scope for argument. Merritt's information was from Major Stanton, substantially to the effect that eight hundred Cheyenne warriors would leave the reservation on Sunday morning, fully equipped for the war-path, and with the avowed intention of joining the hostiles in the Big Horn country. To continue on his march to Laramie, and let them go, would have been gross, if not criminal, neglect. To follow by the direct road to the reservation, sixty-five miles away, would have been simply to drive them out and hasten their move. Manifestly there was but one thing to be done; to throw himself across their path and capture or drive them back, and to do this he must, relatively speaking, march over three sides of a square while they were traversing the fourth, *and must do it undiscovered.*

If Merritt hesitated ten minutes, his most intimate associates, his staff, did not know it. Leaving a small guard with the wagon train, and ordering Lieutenant Hall to catch up with us at night, the General and seven companies swing into saddle, and at one o'clock are marching up the Rawhide, *away* from the reservation, and with no apparent purpose of interfering in any project, howsoever diabolical, that aboriginal fancy can suggest. We halt a brief half-hour under the Peak, fourteen miles away, water our thirsty horses in the clear, running stream, then remount, and, following our chief, lead away northwestward. By five P.M. we are heading square to the north; at sunset we are descending into the wide valley of the Niobrara, and just at ten P.M. we halt and unsaddle under the tall buttes of the Running Water, close by our old camp at Cardinal's Chair. Only thirty-five miles by the way we came, but horses must eat to live, and we have nothing but the buffalo grass to offer them. We post strong guards and pickets to prevent surprise and scatter our horses well out over the hillsides to pick up all they can. Captain Hayes and I are detailed as officers of the guard and pickets for the night and take our selves off accordingly. At midnight Lieutenant Hall arrives with his long wagon train. At three A.M., in the starlight, Merritt arouses his men; coffee and bacon are hurriedly served; the horses get a good breakfast of oats from the wagons, and at five A.M. we are climbing out of the valley to the north. And now, *Messieurs les Cheyennes,* we'll see who first will bivouac tonight upon the War Bonnet. You are but twenty-eight miles from it; we are fifty to the point where your great trail crosses the little stream. The Sioux, in their picturesque nomenclature, called it after the gorgeous headpiece of beadwork, plume, and eagles' feathers, they wear in battle, the prized war bonnet. The frontiersman, scorning the poetic, considers that he has fittingly, practically, anyway, translated it into Hat Creek; and even for such a name as this, three insignificant creeks within a few miles of one another claim precedence—and Indian and Horsehead creeks are placidly willing to share it with them.

The sun rises over the broad lands of the Sioux to the eastward as we leave the shadowy Niobrara behind. Merritt's swift-stepping gray at the head of the column keeps us on our mettle to save our distance, and the horses answer gamely to the pressing knees of their riders. At 10:15 we sight the palisade fortifications of the infantry company which guards the spring at the head of old Sage Creek, and Lieutenant Taylor eagerly welcomes us. Here, officers, men, and horses take a hurried but substantial lunch. We open fresh boxes of ammunition and cram belts and pockets until every man is loaded like a deep-sea diver and fairly bristles with deadly missiles. Then on we go. East-northeast over

the rolling, treeless prairie, and far to our right and rear
runs the high, rock-faced ridge that shuts out the cold north
winds from the reservation. The day is hot; we are following the Black Hills road, and the dust rises in heavy clouds
above us. But 'tis a long, long way to the Indian crossing,
and we *must* be the first to reach it. At sunset a winding belt
of green in a distant depression marks the presence of a
stream. At eight P.M., silently under the stars, we glide in
among the timbers. At nine the seven companies are unsaddled and in bivouac close under the bluffs, where a little
plateau, around which the creek sweeps in almost complete circle, forms excellent defensive lair, secure against
surprise. We have marched eighty-five miles in thirty-one
hours, and here we are, square in their front, ready and
eager to dispute with the Cheyennes their crossing on the
morrow.

No fires are lighted, except a few tiny blazes in deep-dug
holes, whence no betraying flame may escape. Horses and
men, we bivouac in a great circle along the steep banks of a
sluggish stream. The stars shine brightly overhead, but in the
timber the darkness is intense. Mason, my captain, and I are
just unstrapping our blankets and preparing for a nap, when
Lieutenant Forbush, then adjutant of the regiment, stum-
bles over a fallen tree, and announces that Company "K"
is detailed for guard and picket. I had "been on" all the night
before with Captain Hayes and would gladly have had a
sound sleep before the morrow's work; but when Mason,
after reporting for orders to General Merritt, comes back
and tells me that I am to have command of the outposts
to the southeast, the direction from which the foe must
come, there is compensation in the supposed mistake in
the roster.

We grope out in the darkness, and post our pickets in

hollows and depressions, where, should the bivouac be approached over the distant ridges, they can best observe objects against the sky. The men are tired; and, as they cannot walk post and keep awake, the utmost vigilance is enjoined on noncommissioned officers. Hour after hour I prowl around among the sentries, giving prompt answer to the muffled challenge that greets me with unvarying watchfulness. At one o'clock Colonel Mason and I, making the rounds together, come suddenly upon a post down among the willows next the stream, and are not halted; but we find the sentinel squatting under the bank, only visible in the starlight, apparently dozing. Stealing upon him from behind, I seize his carbine, and the man springs to his feet. Mason sternly rebukes him for his negligence, and is disposed to order him under guard; but old Sergeant Schreiber, who was never known to neglect a duty in his life, declares that he and the sentry were in conversation, and watching together some object across the stream not half a minute before we came upon them. Everywhere else along our front we find the men alert and watchful. At three o'clock the morning grows chilly, and the yelping of the coyotes out over the prairie is incessant. My orders are to call the General at half-past three; and, making my way through the slumbering groups, I find him rolled in his blanket at the foot of a big cottonwood, sleeping "with one eye open," for he is wide awake in an instant, and I return to my outpost towards the southeast.

Outlined against the southern sky is a high ridge, some two miles away. It sweeps around from our left front, where it is lost among the undulations of the prairie. Square to the northeast, some twenty miles distant, the southernmost masses of the Black Hills are tumbled up in sharp relief agains the dawn. A faint blush is stealing along the orient; the ridge line grows darker against the brightening sky; stars overhead are paling, and the boughs of the cottonwoods murmur soft response to the stir of the morning breeze. Objects near at hand no longer baffle our tired eyes, and the faces of my comrades of the guard look drawn and wan in the cold light. We are huddled along a slope which did well enough for night watching; but, as the lay of the land becomes more distinct, we discern, four hundred yards farther out to the southeast, a little conical mound rising from a wave of prairie parallel to our front but shutting off all sight of objects between it and the distant range of heights, so I move my outpost quickly to the new position, and there we find unobstructed view.

To our rear is the line of bluffs that marks the tortuous course of the stream, and the timber itself is now becoming mistily visible in the morning light. A faint wreath of fog creeps up from the stagnant water where busy beavers have checked its flow, and from the southward not even an Indian eye could tell that close under those bluffs seven companies of veteran cavalry are crouching, ready for a spring.

Turning to the front again, I bring my glasses to bear on the distant ridge, and sweep its face in search of moving objects. Off to the right I can mark the trail down which we came the night before, but not a soul is stirring. At half-past four our horses, saddled and bridled, are cropping the bunches of buffalo grass in the "swale" behind us; the four men of the picket are lying among them, lariat in hand. Corporal Wilkinson and I, prone upon the hilltop, are eagerly scanning the front, when he points quickly to the now plainly lighted ridge, exclaiming:

"Look, Lieutenant—there are Indians!"

Another minute, and two miles away we sight another group of five or six mounted warriors. In ten minutes we have seen half a dozen different parties popping up into plain sight, then rapidly scurrying back out of view. At five o'clock they have appeared all along our front for a distance of three miles, but they do not approach nearer. Their movements puzzle me. We do not believe they have seen us. They make no attempt at concealment from our side, but they keep peering over ridges towards the west and dodging behind slopes that hide them from that direction.

General Merritt has been promptly notified of their appearance, and at 5:15 he and General Carr and two or three of the staff ride out under cover of our position, and, dismounting, crawl up beside us and level their glasses.

"What can they be after? What are they watching?" is the question. The Black Hills road is off there somewhere, but no travel is possible just now, and all trains are warned back at Taylor's camp. At half-past five the mystery is solved. Four miles away to the southwest, to our right front, the white covers of army wagons break upon our astonished view. It must be our indefatigable Quartermaster Hall with our train, and he has been marching all night to reach us. He is guarded by two companies of stalwart infantry, but they are invisible. He has stowed them away in wagons, and is probably only afraid that the Indians won't attack him. Wagon after wagon, the white covers come gleaming into sight far over the rolling prairie, and by this time the ridge is swarming with war parties of Cheyennes. Here you are, beggarly, treacherous rascals; for years you have eaten of our bread, lived on our bounty. You are well fed, well cared for; you, your papooses and ponies are fat and independent; but you have heard of the grand revel in blood, scalps, and trophies of your brethren, the Sioux. It is no fight of yours. You have no grievance; but the love of rapine and warfare is the ruling passion, and you must take a hand against the Great Father, whom your treaty binds you to obey and honor. And now you have stuffed your wallets with his rations, your pouches with heavy loads of his best metallic cartridges, all too confidingly supplied you by peace-loving agents, who (for a consideration) wouldn't suspect you of warlike designs for any consideration. You are only a day's march from the reservation; and here, you think, are your first rich victims—a big train going to the Black Hills unguarded. No wonder you circle your swift ponies to the left in eager signals to your belated brethren to come on, come on. In half an hour you'll have five hundred here, and the fate of those teamsters and that train is sealed.

"Have the men had coffee?" asks General Merritt, after a leisurely survey. "Yes, sir," is the adjutant's report. "Then let them saddle up and close in mass under the bluffs," is the order, and General Carr goes off to execute it.

The little hill on which we are lying is steep, almost precipitous on its southern slope, washed away apparently by the torrent that in the rainy season must come tearing down the long ravine directly ahead of us; it leads down from the distant ridge and sweeps past us to our right, where it is crossed by the very trail on which we marched in, and along which, three miles away, the wagon train is now approaching. The two come together like a V, and we are at its point, while between them juts out a long spur of hills. The trail cannot be seen from the ravine, and vice versa, while we on our point see both. At the head of the ravine, a mile and a half away, a party of thirty or forty Indians are scurrying about in eager and excited motion. "What in thunder are those vagabonds fooling about?" says Buffalo Bill, who has joined us with Tait and Chips, two of his pet assistants. Even while we speculate, the answer is plain. Riding towards us, away ahead of the wagon train, two soldiers come loping along the trail. They bring despatches to the command, no doubt, and knowing us to be down here in the bottom somewhere, have started ahead to reach us. They see no Indians; for it is only from them and the train the wily foe is concealed, and all unsuspicious of their danger they come jauntily ahead. Now is the valiant red man's opportunity. Come on, Brothers Swift Bear, Two Bulls, Bloody Hand; come on, ten or a dozen of you, my braves—there are only two of the pale-faced dogs, and they shall feel the red man's vengeance forthwith. Come on, come on! We'll dash down this ravine, a dozen of us, and six to one we'll slay and scalp them without danger to ourselves; and a hundred to one we will brag about it the rest of our natural lives. Only a mile away come our couriers; only a mile and a half up the ravine a murderous party of Cheyennes lash their excited ponies into eager gallop, and down they come towards us.

"By Jove! General," says Buffalo Bill, sliding backwards down the hill, "Now's our chance. Let our party mount here out of sight, and we'll cut those fellows off."

"Up with you, then!" is the answer. "Stay where you are, King. Watch them till they are close under you; then give the word. Come down, every other man of you!"

I am alone on the little mound. Glancing behind me, I see Cody, Tait, and Chips with five cavalrymen, eagerly bending forward in their saddles, grasping carbine and rifle, every eye bent upon me in breathless silence, watching for the signal. General Merritt and Lieutenants Forbush and Pardee are crouching below me. Sergeant Schreiber and Corporal Wilkinson, on all fours, are halfway down the northern slope. Not a horse or man of us visible to the Indians. Only my hatless head and the double fieldglass peer

32

over the grassy mound. Half a mile away are our couriers, now rapidly approaching. Now, my Indian friends, what of you? Oh, what a stirring picture you make as once more I fix my glasses on you! Here, nearly four years after, my pulses bound as I recall the sight. Savage warfare was never more beautiful than in you. On you come, your swift, agile ponies springing down the winding ravine, the rising sun gleaming on your trailing war bonnets, on silver armlets, necklace, gorget; on brilliant painted shield and beaded legging; on naked body and beardless face, stained most vivid vermilion. On you come, lance and rifle, pennon and feather glistening in the rare morning light, swaying in the wild grace of your peerless horsemanship; nearer, till I mark the very ornament on your leader's shield. And on, too, all unsuspecting, come your helpless prey. I hold vengeance in my hand, but not yet to let it go. Five seconds too soon, and you can wheel about and escape us; one second too late, and my blue-coated couriers are dead men. On you come, savage, hungry-eyed, merciless. Two miles behind you are your scores of friends, eagerly, applaudingly watching your exploit. But five hundred yards ahead of you, coolly, vengefully awaiting you are your unseen foes, beating you at your own game; and you are running slap into them. Nearer and nearer—your leader, a gorgeous-looking fellow, on a bounding gray, signals "Close and follow." Three hundred yards more, my buck, and (you fancy) your gleaming knives will tear the scalps of our couriers. Twenty seconds, and you will dash round that point with your war whoop ringing in their ears. Ha! Lances, is it? You don't want your shots heard back at the train. What will you think of ours? "All ready, General?"

"All ready, King. Give the word when you like."

Not a man but myself knows how near they are. Two hundred yards now, and I can hear the panting of of their wiry steeds. A hundred and fifty! That's right—close in, you beggars! Ten seconds more and you are on them! A hundred and twenty-five yards—a hundred—ninety—

"Now, lads, in with you!"

Crash go the hoofs! There's a rush, a wild, ringing cheer; then bang, bang, bang! And in a cloud of dust Cody and his men tumble in among them. General Merritt springs up to my side, Corporal Wilkinson to his. Cool as a cucumber, the Indian leader reins in his pony in sweeping circle to the left, ducks on his neck as Wilkinson's bullet whistles by his head; then *under* his pony, and his return shot "zips" close by the General's cheek. Then comes the cry, "Look to the front; look, look!" and, swarming down the ridge as far as we can see, come dozens of Indian warriors at top speed to the rescue. "Send up the first company!" is Merritt's order as he springs into saddle, and, followed by his adjutant, rides off to the left and front. I jump for my horse, and the vagabond, excited by the shots and rush around us, plunges at his lariat and breaks to the left. As I catch him, I see Buffalo Bill closing on a superbly accoutred warrior. It is the work of a minute; the Indian has fired and missed. Cody's bullet tears through the rider's leg, into his pony's heart, and they tumble in confused heap on the prairie. The Cheyenne struggles to his feet for another shot, but Cody's second bullet crashes through his brain, and the young chief, Yellow Hand, drops lifeless in his tracks.

Here comes my company, "K," trotting up from the bluffs, Colonel Mason at their head, and I take my place in front of my platoon, as, sweeping over the ridge, the field lies before us. Directly in front, a mile away, the redskins are rushing down to join their comrades; and their triumphant yells change to cries of warning as Company "K's" blue line shoots up over the divide.

"Drive them, Mason, but look out for the main ridge," is the only order we hear; and, without a word, shout, or shot, "K" goes squarely at the foe. They fire wildly, wheeling about and backing off towards the hills; but our men waste no shot, and we speed up the slope, spreading out unconsciously in open order to right and left. Their bullets whistle harmlessly over our heads, and some of our young men are eagerly looking for permission to begin. Now the pursued have opened fire from both our flanks, for we have spread them open in our rush; and, glancing over my shoulder, it is glorious to see Montgomery's beautiful grays sweeping to our right and rear, while Kellogg's men are coming "front into line" at the gallop on our left. We gain the crest only to find the Indians scattering like chaff before us, utterly confounded at their unexpected encounter. Then comes the pursuit—a lively gallop over rolling prairie, the Indians dropping blankets, rations, everything weighty they could spare except their guns and ammunition. Right and left, far and near, they scatter into small bands and go tearing homeward. Once within the limits of the reservation they are safe, and we strain every nerve to catch them; but when the sun is high in the heavens and noon has come, the Cheyennes are back under the sheltering wing of the Indian Bureau, and not one of them can we lay hands on.

Baffled and astounded, for once in a lifetime beaten at their own game, their project of joining Sitting Bull nipped in the bud, they mourn the loss of three of their best braves slain in sudden attack, and of all their provender and supplies lost in hurried flight. Weary enough we reach the agency building at seven that evening, disappointed at having bagged no greater game; but our chief is satisfied. Buffalo Bill is radiant; his are the honors of the day; and the Fifth generally goes to sleep on the ground, well content with the affair on the War Bonnet.

FOUR

THE MARCH TO THE BIG HORN

CHASING THE CHEYENNES from the War Bonnet and Indian Creek to the reservation, our seven companies had struck cross country, and until we neared the high bluffs and ridges to the north of the agency, it was not difficult for the wagons to follow us; but it was generally predicted that Lieutenant Hall would never be able to get his train over the ravines and "breaks" which he would encounter on the 18th, and the command was congratulating itself on the prospect of a day's rest at Red Cloud, when at noon, to our utter astonishment, the wagons hove in sight. We had fasted since our four o'clock breakfast on the previous morning— were hungrily eying the Indian supplies in their plethoric storehouses, and were just about negotiating with the infantry men of Camp Robinson for the loan of rations and the wherewithal to cook the same, when Hall rode in, nonchalant as usual, and parked his train of supplies amid shouts of welcome. General Merritt was unfeignedly glad to see his quartermaster; he had received his orders to hasten in to Fort Laramie and proceed to the reinforcement of General Crook, and every moment was precious. We were allowed just two hours to prepare and partake of an ample dinner, pack our traps and store them in the wagons again, when "boots and saddles" was echoed back from the white crags of Dancer's Hill and Crow Butte, and at 2:30 we were winding up the beautiful valley of the White River. Lieutenant Hall was left with his train to give his teams and teamsters a needed rest, and ordered to follow us at early evening.

All the morning the reservation Indians had come in flocks to have a look at the soldiers who had outwitted them on the previous day. Arrapahoe and Ogalalla, Minneconjou and Uncapapa, represented by dozens of old chiefs and groups of curious and laughing squaws, hung about us for hours—occasionally asking questions and invariably professing a readiness to accept any trifle we might feel disposed to part with. To beg is the one thing of which an Indian is never ashamed. In Arizona I have known a lot of Apaches to hang around camp for an entire day, and when they had coaxed us out of our last plug of tobacco, our only remaining match, and our old clothes, instead of going home satisfied they would turn to with reviving energy and beg for the things of all others for which they had not the faintest use—soap and writing paper.

In addition to all the "squaw men" and "blanket Indians" at the reservation, there came to see us that day quite a number of Cheyennes, our antagonists of the day before. Shrouded in their dark blue blankets and washed clean of their lurid war paint, they were by no means imposing. One and all they wanted to see Buffalo Bill, and wherever he moved they followed him with awe-filled eyes. He wore the same dress in which he had burst upon them in yesterday's fight, a Mexican costume of black velvet, slashed with scarlet and trimmed with silver buttons and lace—one of his theatrical garbs, in which he had done much execution before the footlights in the States, and which now became of intensified value. Bill had carefully preserved the beautiful war bonnet, shield and decorations, as well as the arms of the young chieftain Yellow Hand, whom he had slain in single combat, and that winter ('76 and '77) was probably the most profitable of his theatrical career. The incidents of the fight of the 17th and the death of Yellow Hand were dramatized for him, and presented one of the most telling of the plays in which he starred all over the East that season. He realized above all expenses some $13,000 on that one alone, and I fancy that some of your readers may have seen it. For a time it was his custom to display the trophies of that fight in some prominent show window during the day, and take them away only in time for the performance at night. As an advertisement it drew largely in the West, but when Bill reached the refinements of the Middle States and the culture of New England he encountered a storm of abuse from the press and the clergy which, while it induced him to withdraw "the blood-stained trophies of his murderous and cowardly deeds" from the show windows, so stimulated public curiosity as to materially augment his receipts.

It is in New England, the land of the Pequots and the Iroquois, that the most violent partisans of the peace policy are to be found today. There is method in their cultured mania, for the farther removed the citizen finds himself from the Indian the better he likes him. Year after year, with the westward march of civilization, the Indian has found himself, in the poetic and allegorical language ascribed to him by Cooper and others who never heard him use it, "thrust farther towards the fiery bosom of the setting sun." Each state in turn has elbowed him on towards the Mississippi, and by the time the struggling aborigine was at the safe distance of two or three states away, was virtuously ready to preach fierce denunciation of the people who simply did as it had done. It is comical today to hear Mr. Conger of

Michigan assailing Mr. Belford of Colorado because the latter considers it time for the Utes to move or become amenable to the laws of the land; and when we look back and remember how the whole movement was inaugurated by the Pilgrim Fathers, is it not edifying to read the Bostonian tirades against the settlers—the pilgrims and pioneers of the Far West?

Our march to Laramie was without noteworthy incident. We reached the North Platte on Friday afternoon, July 21, spent Saturday in busy preparation, and early Sunday morning, six o'clock, the trumpets were sounding "the General," the universal army signal to strike your tent and march away. The white canvas was folded into the wagons, and in a few moments more the column of horse was moving off on the long-anticipated march to join General Crook. Captain Egan and Lieutenant Allison of the Second Cavalry rode out from Laramie to wish us Godspeed. By eight the sun was scorching our backs and great clouds of dust were rising under our horses' feet, and Laramie was left behind. Many and many a weary march, many a week of privation and suffering, many a stirring scene were we to encounter before once again the hospitable old frontier fort would open its gates to receive us. At half-past two we camped along the Platte at Bull Bend, and had a refreshing bath in its rapid waters; at four a violent storm of wind and rain bore down upon us, and beat upon our canvas during the night, but morning broke all the better for marching. A cold drizzle is far preferable to thick dust. We sped along briskly to the "La Bonté," and from there hastened on to Fetterman, where the main command arrived at noon on the 25th, the wagons and rear guard, of which I was in charge, coming in two hours later, fording the Platte at once, and moving into camp some distance upstream.

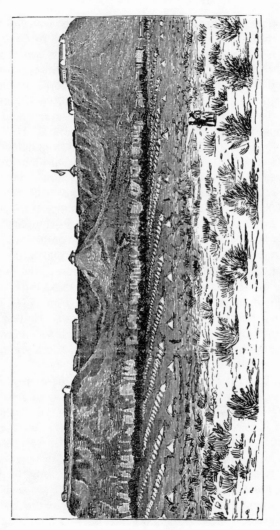

Fort Fetterman

Fetterman was crowded with wagon trains, new horses, recruits, and officers, all waiting to go forward to General Crook, north of the Big Horn, and with eight companies of the Fifth Cavalry as a nucleus, General Merritt organized the array of "unattached" into a disciplined force, brought chaos into prompt subjection, and at eight A.M. on the 26th started the whole mass on its northward march. Among those to meet us here were our old Arizona comrades, Lieutenants Rodgers and Eaton, who had hurried from detached service to catch us, and there were some comical features in the reunion. They had escaped from Eastern cities but the week previous, had made the journey by rail to Cheyenne and Medicine Bow, and by stage or ambulance to Fetterman, were fresh and trim and neat as though stepping out for parade. We had been marching and scouting for six weeks through scorching dust and alkali, and with untrimmed beards and begrimed attire were unrecognizable. Rodgers positively refused to believe in the identity of a comrade whom he had met at a german at Fort Hays, but forgot his scruples when he received through that same officer the notification that he was promoted to the command of Company "A," its captain having suddenly concluded to resign a short time before.

Here, too, the future medical director of the expedition, Dr. Clements, made his appearance, and joined for the campaign, and two officers of the Fourth Infantry, whose companies were not included in General Crook's field force, obtained authority to serve with the Fifth Cavalry. And among those who cast their lot with us as volunteers there came a gallant sailor, a lieutenant of our navy, who, having leave of absence from his department after long sea service, came out to spend a portion thereof in hunting on the Plains, just as his cousin, Lieutenant Rodgers, was hastening to join his regiment; and Jack Tar became a cavalry man, to serve for three months of the war, and it wasn't a week before Mr. Hunter had won the regard of every officer and man in the Fifth, and the brevet of "Commodore," by which title he was universally hailed throughout the long and dreary campaign that followed.

Two more companies of ours, "E" and "F," had been ordered to join us also, but we were in a hurry, and they followed by forced marches. On the night of the 28th we were encamped in pitchy darkness in a narrow valley at the headwaters of the North Fork of the Muni Pusa. I was aroused from sleep by the voice of Lieutenant Pardee, who was serving as an aide-de-camp to General Merritt, and, rolling out of my blankets, found the general and himself at our tent. They asked if we had heard the distant sound of cavalry trumpets. The General thought he had, and we all went out beyond the post of the sentinels upon the open prairie to listen. It was time for Captains Price and Payne to reach us with their companies, and the General thought that in the thick darkness they had lost the trail and were signalling in hopes of a reply, and so we pricked up our ears. The silence was as dense as the darkness; no sound came from the slumbering camp; no light from the smouldering fire; suddenly there floated throught the night air, soft and clear, the faint notes of the cavalry trumpet sounding "Officer's Call"; another minute and it was answered by our chief trumpeter, and, guided by the calls, in half an hour our comrades had joined us, and ten companies of the Fifth Cavalry were camped together for the first time in years.

From that night "Officer's Call" grew to be the conventional signal by which we of the Fifth were wont to herald our coming through the darkness or distance to comrades

43

who might be awaiting us. Last September, when the Utes made their attack on Major Thornburgh's command, your readers will doubtless remember that after that gallant soldier's death the command of the besieged battalion devolved upon Captain Payne of the Fifth Cavalry. He and his company, who were the first to employ the signal, have best reason to remember its subsequent value; and I cannot do better than to repeat in his own words my classmate's description of the arrival of General Merritt and the regiment after their famous dash of two hundred miles to the rescue. Of his little battalion of three companies, fifty were lying wounded in the hurriedly constructed rifle pits—he and his surgeon were of the number—and for six days the Indians had poured in a pitiless fire whenever hand or head became visible. Hoping for the speedy coming of his colonel, Payne tells us: "While lying in the trenches on the night of the 4th of October, this incident came to mind. Believing it *just* possible for General Merritt to reach us next morning, and knowing that, if possible, come he would, I directed one of my trumpeters to be on the alert for the expected signal. And so it was; just as the first gray of the dawn appeared, our listening ears caught the sound of "Officer's Call" breaking the silence of the morning, and filling the valley with the sweetest music we had ever heard. Joyously the reply rang out from our corral, and the men rushing from the rifle pits made the welkin ring with their glad cheers."

First at the headwaters of the Mini Pusa, in July, '76; last in the valley of the Milk River. Next? Far out in the cañons of Colorado, utterly isolated from the world, snowed in, living we don't know how, four companies of the Fifth Cavalry are waiting at the ruins of the White River Agency the result of all this negotiation in Washington. Merritt with the other companies, six in number, is wintering at Fort

Russell, on the line of the Union Pacific. More than probable is it that the earliest spring will find him a second time making that two-hundred-mile march to the Milk River, and once again the Rockies will echo the stirring strains of "Officer's Call."

Saturday, the 29th of July, '76, broke like a morning in mid-Sahara. We marched in glaring sun through miles of dust, sagebrush, and alkali, and followed it up on Sunday, the 30th, with just such another; no shade, no grass, no water fit to swallow. We bivouacked along the Powder River, a curdling stream the color of dirty chalk, and we gazed with wistful, burning eyes at the grand peaks of the Big Horn, mantled with glistening snow, only fifty miles away. Monday was another day of heat, glare, and dust, with that tantalizing glory of ice and snow twenty miles nearer. That night the wind started in from the west and blew down from those very peaks, fanning our fevered cheeks like blessed wavelets from heaven, as indeed they were. We were gasping for air on the banks of Crazy Woman's Fork, and would have suffocated but for that glad relief.

Early next morning Merritt led us on again, marching through a rolling country that became more and more varied and interesting with every mile; we were edging in closer to the foothills of the mountains. Several small herds of buffalo were sighted, and some few officers and men were allowed to go with Cody in chase. At one P. M. we halted on Clear Fork, a beautiful running stream deserving of its name, fresh from the snow peaks on our left, had lunch and rested until five, when once more we saddled up and pushed ahead; came suddenly upon Lake De Smet, wild and picturesque, lying like a mirror in a deep basin of treeless banks; and in a beautiful open glade, rich with abundant green grass and watered by a clear, cold rivulet, we camped in the glorious starlight, thanking Heaven we were out of the desert, and at last along the storied range of the Big Horn.

Wednesday, August 2d, dawned bracing, clear, and beautiful. The glorious sunshine beamed on lofty crags and pine-covered heights close at our left hand, peered into dark ravine and rocky gorge, sparkled on the swift-flowing stream, and on innumerable dewdrops over the glade. Men and horses awoke to new life. A few miles ahead lay a lofty ridge, and from that, said our guides, the valleys of the Tongue and its branches, and the grand sweep of country towards the Rosebud on the north and the Big Horn River to the northwest would be spread before us like a map. Over that ridge, somewhere, lies Crook with his force, expectant of our coming; over that ridge, beyond him, are or were ten thousand renegades and hostile Indians, Sioux, and San Arcs, Cheyennes of the North (it was the Southern Cheyennes we whipped back on the War Bonnet), Minneconjous, Uncapapas (Sitting Bull's Own), Yanktonnais, and Brulés, all banded together in one grand attempt to exterminate the white intruders.

How I envied the advance that day the first glimpse over that divide! But each company took its turn at head of column; and now that we were fairly in among the fastnesses, where attack might be expected at any moment, two companies were daily detailed to escort and guard the wagon train, and Companies "A" and "K" were the unfortunates today. It was mean duty. The road was not bad, but it wound up and down, over crests and through deep ravines. We had to dismount and lend a helping hand half the time. At seven we passed the palisaded ruins of old Fort Phil Kearney [Kearny], abandoned by "Peace Commission" order in '68; and just beyond we halted and silently surveyed the ridge on which Captains Fetterman and Brown, Lieutenant Grummond, and three companies of soldiers were slowly slaughtered by Red Cloud and his surrounding thousands in December, '66. We fancied the poor women and children in the fort, listening and looking on in dumb, helpless horror; and then we thought of Custer and his comrades lying yet unburied only a few miles farther across that uplifted barrier in our front, and then we hurried on, eagerly praying that it might be our fortune to avenge some of those sacrificed lives; toiled up the long, long ascent, reached the lofty crest, and halted again in sheer amaze. The whole landscape to the north was black with smoke. East, as far as the Cheetish (Wolf) Mountains; west, as far as the Little Horn, from every valley great masses of surging, billowy clouds rolled up to swell the pall that overspread the northern sky and hung low upon the dividing ridges towards the Yellowstone. Here and there forked flames shot up through the heated veil, and even at our distance we could almost hear their roar and crackle. "Lo" had set the country afire to baffle his pursuers, and, knowing of the coming of Crook's reinforcements, was now, in all probability, scattering over the continent.

At eleven we passed an abandoned outpost of earthworks —thrown up, probably, by a detached company guarding the road. At two we overtook Merritt and the eight companies resting along a cool, limpid stream that gave promise of trout; and here we camped for the night and listened eagerly to the news brought us by courier from General Crook. Scouts were out hunting for the Indians, who had withdrawn their masses from his immediate front, and he was only waiting our coming to launch out in pursuit. We sleep that night restless and impatient of the delay—morning comes all too slowly—but at four o'clock we are astir

47

and on the move to meet our brigadier, but couriers report him coming down towards us along the main valley of the Tongue. We unsaddle and wait till three in the afternoon, when again "the General" sounds, and we march north-wardly over the ridges towards the thick smoke. "Crook is camping on Goose Creek," is the explanation, and we are to join him there. At half-past five we catch glimpses of distant patrols and herds of cavalry horses and quartermasters' mules on the sloping sidehills. Presently horsemen come cantering out to meet us. Gray-haired, handsome, soldierly as ever, the first to hail us is our old Arizona major, now Lieutenant Colonel Royall of the Third Cavalry—with him a group of his own and the Second Cavalry officers. But we are still moved onward. We descend a long spur of foothill, plunge through a rapid mountain torrent into dense timber on the other side, still guided by our welcoming comrades, ride with dripping flanks through willow and cottonwood into brilliant light beyond. There white tent and wagon covers gleam in every direction; rough, bearded men are shouting greeting; and just ahead, on the trail, in worn shooting jacket, slouch felt hat, and soldier's boots, with ragged beard braided and tied with tape, with twinkling eyes and half-shy, embarrassed manner, stands our old Arizona friend and chieftain, the hardworking soldier we have come all these many miles to join, looking as natural as when we last saw him in the spurs of the Sierras. There is no mistaking the gladness of his welcome. His face lights up with new light. He has a cordial word with General Carr, who commands the leading battalion; then turns to me, and with a grasp of the hand that fairly makes me wince, gives greeting for which I'd make that march twice over.

FIVE

THE ASSEMBLY OF THE B. H. AND Y.

FRIDAY, the 4th of August, 1876, was a busy day in the camp of General Crook. He had been waiting impatiently for the coming of the Fifth Cavalry in order that he might resume the offensive, and, to use his own words, "finish the campaign in one crushing blow." The tragic success of the Indians on the Little Big Horn, of June 25th, resulting in the annihilation of Custer and five companies of the Seventh Cavalry, compelled General Terry to fall back to the Yellowstone, where he set about the reorganization of his command; and, safely intrenched in his supply camp at the mouth of the Tongue River, he too had been awaiting the arrival of reinforcements. General Miles with his fine regiment, the Fifth Infantry, was hurried up the Missouri from Fort Leavenworth, and companies of the twenty-second Infantry, from the Lakes, also hastened to join him. They were stemming the muddy current of the great river as fast as the light-draft steamers could carry them, while we were marching up from Fetterman to join General Crook.

On the 4th of August, Terry's command, consisting of the remnant of the seventh Cavalry, one battalion of the Second Cavalry, the Fifth Infantry (Miles), Seventh Infantry (Gibbon), a battalion of the Twenty-second, and the Sixth Infantry garrison at Fort Buford, threatened the hostiles on the side of the Yellowstone; while General

Crook, with the entire Third Cavalry, ten companies of the Fifth, and four of the Second Cavalry, and an admirable infantry command, consisting of detachments from the Fourth, Ninth, and Fourteenth regiments, was preparing to advance upon them from the south. The two armies were not more than one hundred and twenty-five miles apart, yet communication between them was impossible. The intervening country swarmed with warriors, six to eight thousand in number, completely armed, equipped, supplied, and perfectly mounted. Crook had sallied forth and fought them on the 17th of June and found them altogether too strong and dexterous, so he retired to Goose Creek once more; and here he lay on the 25th of June, when Custer was making his attack and meeting his fate—only fifty miles away, and not a soul of our command had the faintest idea of what was going on.

Warily watching the two commands, the Indians lay uneasily between Crook and Terry. Noting the approach of strong reinforcements to both, they proceeded to get their women and children out of the way, sending them eastward across Terry's front, and preparing to do likewise themselves when the time came for them to start. On the 5th of August the two armies moved towards each other. On the 10th they met; and one of the most comical sights I ever witnessed was this meeting, and one of the most unanswerable questions ever asked was, "Why, where on earth are the Indians?"

However, August the 4th was a day of busy preparation. At ten A.M. the regimental and battalion commanders met in council at General Crook's headquarters, and by noon the result of their deliberations was promulgated. From the reports of his scouts and allies, General Crook had every reason to believe that he would find the mass of Indians

Supply Camp, Head of Tongue River

posted in strong force somewhere among the bluffs and uplands of the Rosebud, two days' march away to the north. He had been unable to hear from General Terry or to communicate with him. Lieutenant Sibley, of the Second Cavalry, a young officer of great ability, and universally conceded to be as full of cool courage as any man could well be, had made a daring attempt to slip through with thirty picked men; but the Indians detected him quick as a flash, and after a desperate fight he managed to get back to the command with most of his men, but with the loss of all his horses.

The organization of the command was announced at one P.M.: General Crook to command in person, his faithful aide-de-camp, Bourke, to act as adjutant-general, while his staff consisted of Lieutenant Schuyler, Fifth Cavalry, junior aide-de-camp; Dr. B. A. Clements, medical director, assisted by Drs. Hartsuff and Patzki; Major J. V. Furey, chief quartermaster; Captain J. W. Bubb, chief commissary; Major George M. Randall, chief of scouts and Indian allies; and the bloodthirsty paymaster, our old friend Major Stanton, was the general utility man.

The cavalry was organized as a brigade, with General Merritt in command—Lieutenants Forbush and Hall, Fifth Cavalry, Pardee and Young, of the infantry, serving as staff. General Carr took command of the Fifth Cavalry, with myself as adjutant; and for the first time the promotions which had occurred in the regiment consequent upon the death of General Custer were recognized in the assignments to command. The commissions had not yet been received from Washington, but all knew the advancement had been made. So my old captain, now become Major Mason, turned over Company "K" to its new captain, Woodson, and was detailed to command the Second Battalion of the Fifth Cav-

alry, consisting of Companies "B," "D," "E," "F," and
"K," while the First Battalion—Companies "A," "C," "G,"
"I," and "M,"—remained, as heretofore, under the leader-
ship of our fellow citizen Major Upham.

The Third Cavalry was commanded by Lieutenant Colonel Royall, under whom also was the battalion of the Second Cavalry. Consequently, it was his distinguished priv-
ilege to issue orders to four battalions, while his senior officer
and quondam commander, Lieutenant Colonel Carr (brevet
major general) had only two. This was a source of much
good-natured raillery and mutual chaffing on the part of
these two veteran campaigners, and it was Royall's ceaseless delight to come over and talk to Carr about "my brigade," and to patronizingly question him about "your a—
detachment." In fact, I believe that Colonel Royall so far
considered his command a brigade organization that his
senior major, Colonel Evans, assumed command of the
Third Cavalry as well as his own battalion; but, as this was
a matter outside of by own sphere of duties, I cannot make
an assertion.

The infantry was a command to be proud of, and Lieutenant Colonel Alexander Chambers was the man to appre-
ciate it. Detachments from three fine regiments gave him
a full battalion of tough, wiry, fellows, who had footed it a
thousand miles that summer, and we were all the better prepared to march two thousand more.

With every expectation of finding our foes close at hand,
General Crook's orders were concise enough. As given to
me by General Carr and recorded in my notebook, I tran-
scribe them here: "All tents, camp equipage, bedding, and
baggage, except articles hereinafter specified, to be stored
in the wagons, and wagons turned over to care of chief
quartermaster by sunrise tomorrow. Each company to have

their coffee roasted and ground and turned over to the chief commissary at sunset tonight. Wagons will be left here at camp. A pack-train of mules will accompany each battalion on the march, for the protection of which the battalion will be held responsible. The regiment will march at seven A.M. tomorrow, 'prepared for action,' and company commanders will see to it that each man carries with him on his person one hundred rounds carbine ammunition and four days' rations, overcoat and one blanket on the saddle. Fifty rounds additional per man will be packed on mules. Four extra horses, not to be packed, will be led with each company. Currycombs and brushes will be left in wagons. *Special instructions for action:* All officers and noncommissioned officers to take constant pains to prevent wastage of ammunition."

That was all. From the General down to subalterns the officers started with no more clothing than they had on and the overcoat and blanket indicated in that order. Many, indeed, officers and men, thinking to be back in a week, left overcoats behind as superfluous in that bright August weather. When I tell you it was ten weeks before we saw those wagons again, meantime the weather having changed from summer sun to mountain storm and sleet, and we having tramped some eight hundred miles, you can fancy what a stylish appearance the Fifth Cavalry—indeed, the whole expedition—presented as it marched into the Black Hills the following September.

Saturday morning, the 5th of August, broke clear and cloudless, and at the very peep of day the hillsides re-echoed to the stirring music of our reveille. Cavalry trumpet, soft and mellow, replied to the deeper tone of the infantry bugle. We of the Fifth tumbled up in prompt and cheery response to the summons. Roll call was quickly over.

The horses took their final grooming with coltish impatience and devoured their grain in blissful ignorance of the sufferings in store for them. The officers gathered for the last time in two months around their mess chests and thankfully partook of a bountiful breakfast. Then "the General" rang out from cavalry headquarters; down fell the snowy canvas in every direction; wagon after wagon loaded up in the rapid style acquired only in long campaigning and trundled off to join the quartermaster's corral. The long column of infantry crawled away northward over the divide; half a dozen mounted scouts and rangers cantered away upon their flanks; the busy packers drove up their herds of braying mules, lashed boxes of hardtack and sacks of bacon upon the snugly-fitting *aparejo*—the only packsaddle that ever proved a complete success—and finally everything was ready for the start. The bustling town of yesterday had disappeared, and only long rows of saddles and bridles disposed upon the turf in front of each company indicated the regimental position.

At General Carr's headquarters, among the willows close to the stream, a white flag, with a centre square of red, is fluttering in the breeze. It is one of the signal flags, but as the regimental standard had been left with the band at Fort Hays, the General adopted this for the double purpose of indicating his own position and of conveying messages to the distant outposts. Yesterday afternoon a group of our Indian allies, Crows and Shoshones, surrounded that flag with wondering interest from the moment of its first appearance. Accustomed to the use of signals themselves, they eagerly watch any improvement upon their system, and, learning from Sergeant Center, our standard bearer and signal sergeant, that this was a "speaking flag," they hung around for hours to observe its operation. The herds of

55

the different companies were browsing on the hillsides half a mile away, strong pickets being thrown out in their front, and each herd guarded by a sergeant and party from its own company. So General Carr, to give the Indians an idea of its use and at the same time secure more room, directed the Sergeant to "Flag those Second Battalion herds to the other side of that ravine." So Center signalled "Attention" to the outposts, to which they waved "22, 22, 22, 3," the signal for "All right, go ahead, we're ready," and then, with the staring eyes of a score of swarthy warriors following his every move, Center rapidly swung his flag to form the message: "General Carr directs herds Second Battalion cross ravine." Speedily the grays of Company "B" and the four bay herds of the other companies began the movement, were slowly guided through the sorrels, blacks, and bays of the First Battalion, and commenced the descent into the ravine. One herd lagged a little behind, and the General, gazing at them through his binocular, quickly divined the cause. "Confound that herd guard; tell 'em to take off those side-lines when they're moving, if it's only a hundred yards." The message is sent as given, the side lines whipped off, the horses step freely to their new grazing ground, Crow and Shoshonee mutter guttural approbation and say that flag is "heap good medicine."

Hours afterwards they are hunting about camp for old flour sacks and the like, and several towels, spread on the bushes at the bathing-place below camp to dry in the sun, are missing.

Now, on this brilliant Saturday morning, as we wait expectant of the signal "Boots and Saddles," the cavalcade of our fierce allies comes spattering and plunging through the stream. Grim old chieftains, with knees hunched up on their ponies' withers, strapping young bucks bedaubed in yellow paint and red, blanketted and busy squaws scurrying around herding the spare ponies, driving the pack animals, "toting" the young, doing all the work in fact. We have hired these hereditary enemies of the Sioux as our savage auxiliaries, "regardless of expense," and now, as they ride along the line, and our irrepressible Mulligans and Flahertys swarm to the fore intent on losing no opportunity for fun and chaff, and the "big Indians" in the lead come grinning and nodding salutations towards the group of officers at headquarters, a general laugh breaks out, for nearly every warrior has decorated himself with a miniature signal flag. Fluttering at the end of his "coup" stick or stuck in his headgear, a small square of white towelling or floursack, with a centre daub of red paint, is displayed to the breeze, and, under his new ensign, Mr. Lo rides complacently along, convinced that he has entered upon his campaign with "good medicine."

Half-past six. Still no signal to bring in the herds. But Merritt, Carr, and Royall are born and bred cavalrymen, and well know the value of every mouthful of the rich dew-laden grass before the march begins. We are exchanging good-byes with the quartermasters and the unhappy creatures who are to remain behind, adding our closing messages to the letters we leave for dear ones in distant homes, when the cheery notes ring out from brigade headquarters and are taken up, repeated along the line by the regimental trumpeters. Far out on the slopes our horses answer with eager hoof and neigh; with springy steps the men hasten out to bridle their steeds, and, vaulting on their backs, ride in by companies to the line. The bustle of saddling, the snap of buckle and whip of cinch, succeeds, then "Lead into line" is heard from the sergeant's lips. Officers ride slowly along their commands, carefully scrutinizing each horse and man.

Blanket, poncho, overcoat, side line, lariat, and picket pin, canteen and haversack, each has its appropriate place and must be in no other. Each trooper in turn displays his "thimble belt" and extra pocket package to show that he has the prescribed one hundred rounds. The adjutant, riding along the line, receives the report of each captain and transfers it to his notebook. Away down the valley we see the Second and Third already in motion, filing off around the bluffs. Then General Carr's chief trumpeter raises his clarion to his lips. "Mount," rings out upon the air, and with the sound twenty officers and five hundred and fifteen men swing into saddle. Ten minutes more and we are winding across the divide towards Prairie Dog Creek on the east. The Third and Second, a mile to our left, are marching northeastward on the trail of the infantry. We fill our lungs with deep draughts of the rare, bracing mountain breeze, take a last glance at the grand crags and buttresses of rock to the southward, then with faces eagerly set towards the rolling smoke wreaths that mark the track of the savage foe in the valley of the "Deje Agie," we close our columns, shake free our bridle reins, and press steadily forward. "Our wild campaign has begun."

SIX

THE MEET ON THE ROSEBUD

THAT GENERAL CROOK'S COMMAND, now designated as the "Big Horn and Yellowstone Expedition," started upon its campiagn in the best possible spirits and under favoring skies, no one who saw us that bright August morning could have doubted. Unhappily, there was no one to see, no one to cheer or applaud; and once having cut loose from our wagons and their guards, there was not a soul to mark our progress, unless it were some lurking scout in distant lair, who trusted to his intimate knowledge of the country and to his pony's fleetness to keep himself out of our clutches. Once fairly in the valley of the Prairie Dog, we had a good look at our array. The Fifth Cavalry in the long column were bringing up the rear on this our first day's march from Goose Creek; our packers and their lively little mules jogging briskly along upon our right flank, while the space between us and the rolling foothills on the left was thickly covered with our Crow allies. The Shoshones were ahead somewhere, and we proceeded to scrape acquaintance with these wild warriors of the far northwest, whom we were now meeting for the first time. Organized in 1855, our regiment had seen its first Indian service on the broad plains of Texas, and was thoroughly well known among the Comanches, Kiowas, and Lipans when the great war of the rebellion broke out. In those days, with Sidney Johnston,

Robert E. Lee, Earl Van Dorn, Kirby Smith, Fitz Hugh Lee, and a dozen others who became notorious in the rebel army as its representative officers, our regiment had been not inaptly styled "Jeff. Davis's Own." But it outgrew the baleful title during the war, and has lost almost every trace of its ante bellum personnel. Two of its most distinguished captains of today—Montgomery and "Jack" Hayes—it is true acquired their earliest military experience in its ranks under those very officers. But, while they are all the better as cavalrymen for that fact, they are none the less determined in their loyalty, and both fought in many a wild charge during the rebellion, defending their flag against the very men who had taught them the use of their sabres. In that stern baptism of blood the Fifth became regenerate, and after stirring service in the Army of the Potomac during the war and throughout the South during Reconstruction days, the regiment once more drifted out on the plains, was introduced to the Cheyennes and Sioux in the winter of 1868–69, became very much at home among the Apaches of Arizona from 1871 to 1875, and now we found ourselves, after a long march across country from the Pacific slope, scraping acquaintance with the redoubtable "Crows" of the Yellowstone Valley, the lifelong enemies of the Sioux.

Riding "at ease," the men talk, laugh, and sing if they want to. All that is required is that they shall not lounge in the saddle, and that they keep accurately their distance, and ride at a steady walk. The Crows are scattered along the entire length of our left flank, but a band of some fifteen or twenty chiefs and headmen keep alongside the headquarters party at the front of column. There rides General Carr with his adjutant, the surgeon, the noncommissioned staff, and orderlies, and, of course, the standard-bearer, who, as previously explained, has a signal flag for this campaign, and it is this which attracts the aborigine.

These Crows are fine-looking warriors, and fine horsemen too; but to see them riding along at ease, their ponies apparently gliding over the ground in their quick, catlike walk, their position in the saddle seems neither graceful nor secure. This knot on our left is full of the most favorable specimens, and they all ride alike. Every man's blanket is so disposed that it covers him from the back of his head, folds across his breast, leaving the arms free play in a manner only an Indian can accomplish, and then is tucked in about his thighs and knees so as to give him complete protection. One or two younger bucks have discarded their blankets for the day, and ride about in dingy calico shirts or old cavalry jackets. One or two also appear in cavalry trousers instead of the native breechclout and legging. But the moment that Indian dismounts you notice two points in which he is diametrically opposed to the customs of his white brother; first, that he mounts and dismounts on the right (off) side of his horse; second, that he carefully cuts out and throws away that portion of a pair of trousers which with us is regarded as indispensable. He rides hunched up in his saddle, with a stirrup so short that his knees are way out to the front and bent in an acute angle. The stirrup itself is something like the shoe of a lady's sidesaddle, and he thrusts his moccasined foot in full length. He carries in his right hand a wooden handle a foot long to which three or four thongs of deerskin are attached, and with this scourge-like implement he keeps up an incessant shower of light flaps upon his pony's flank, rarely striking him heavily; and nothing will convince him that under that system the pony will not cover more miles in a day at a walk or lope than any horse in

America. His horse equipments are of the most primitive description—a light wooden framework or tree, with high, narrow pommel and cantle, much shorter in the seat than ours, the whole covered with hide, stitched with thongs and fastened on with a horsehair girth, constitute his saddle. Any old piece of blanket or coffee sack answers for saddle cloth, and his bridle is the simplest thing in the world, a single headpiece, a light snaffle bit, and a rein, sometimes gayly ornamented, completes the arrangement. But at full speed the worst horseman among them will dash up hill or down, through tortuous and rocky stream beds, everywhere that a goat would go, and he looks upon our boldest rider as a poor specimen.

The Crows are affably disposed today, and we have no especial difficulty in fraternizing. Plug tobacco will go a long way as a medium of introduction anywhere west of the Missouri; and if you give one Indian a piece as big as a postage-stamp, the whole tribe will come in to claim acquaintance. A very pretty tobacco pouch of Sioux manufacture which hung always at the pommel of my saddle and the heavily beaded buckskin riding breeches which I wore seemed to attract their notice, and one of them finally managed to communicate through a half-breed interpreter a query as to whether I had killed the Sioux chief who had owned them. Finding that I had never killed a Sioux in my life, the disdainful warrior dropped me as no longer a desirable acquaintance; and even the fact that the breeches were a valuable present from no less a hero than Buffalo Bill failed to make a favorable impression. Following him were a pair of bright-looking young squaws whose sole occupation in life seemed to consist in ministering to the various wants of his sulky chiefship. Riding astride, just as the men do, these ladies were equally at home on ponyback, and they "herded" his spare "mounts" and drove his pack animals with consummate skill. A tiny papoose hung on the back of one of them, and gazed over her shoulder with solemn, speculative eyes at the long files of soldiers on their tall horses. At that tender age it was in no way compromising his dignity to display an interest in what was going on around him. Later in life he would lose caste as a warrior if he ventured to display wonderment at sight of a flying machine. For several hours we rode side by side with our strange companions. We had no hesitancy in watching them with eager curiosity, and they were as intent on "picking up points" about us, only they did it furtively.

Gradually we were drawing nearer the swift "Deje Agie," as the Crows call the Tongue River. The valley down which we were moving sank deeper among the bold bluffs on either side. Something impeded the march of the column ahead; the pack trains on our right were "doubling up," and every mule, with that strict attention to business characteristic of the species, had buried its nose in the rich buffalo grass, making up for lost time. "Halt!" and "Dismount!" rang out from the trumpets. Every trooper slips the heavy curb bit from his horse's mouth and leads him right or left off the trail that he may profit by even a moment's rest to crop the fresh bunches in which that herbage grows.

The morning has passed without notable incident. No alarm has come from the scouts in front or flank. We are so far in rear today that we miss our friends Cody and Chips, who hitherto were *our* scouts and no one else's. Now they are part and parcel of the squad attached to General Crook's headquarters, of which Major Stanton is the putative chief. We miss our fire-eater of a paymaster—the only one of his corps, I fancy, who would rather undergo the privations of such a campaign and take actual part in its engagements

63

than sit at a comfortable desk at home and criticise its movements. At noon we come suddenly upon the rushing Tongue, and fording breast deep, cross to the northern shore. We emerge at the very base of steep rocky heights, push round a ledge that shuts out the northward prospect from our sight, find the river recoiling from a palisade of rock on the east, and tearing back across our path, ford it again and struggle along under the cliffs on its right bank a few minutes, balancing ourselves, it almost seems, upon a trail barely wide enough for one horseman. What a place for ambuscade or surprise!

We can see no flankers or scouts, but feel confident that our General has not shoved the nose of his column into such a trap without rigid reconnoissance. So we push unconcernedly along. Once more the green, foam-crested torrent sweeps across our line of march from the left, and we ride in, our horses snorting and plunging over the slippery boulders on the bottom, the eager waves dashing up about our knees. Once more we wind around a projecting elbow of bluff, and as the head of our column, which has halted to permit the companies to close up, straightens out in motion again, we enter a beautiful glade. The river, beating in foam against the high, precipitous rocks on the eastern bank, broke in tiny, peaceful wavelets upon the grassy shores and slopes of the western side; the great hills rolled away to the left; groves of timber sprang up in our front, and through their leafy tops the white smoke of many a campfire was curling; the horses of the Second and Third, strongly guarded, were already moving out to graze on the foothills. An aide-de-camp rides to General Carr with orders to "bivouac right here; we march no further today." We ride left into line, unsaddle, and detail our guards. Captain Payne, with Company "F," is assigned the duty of protecting camp

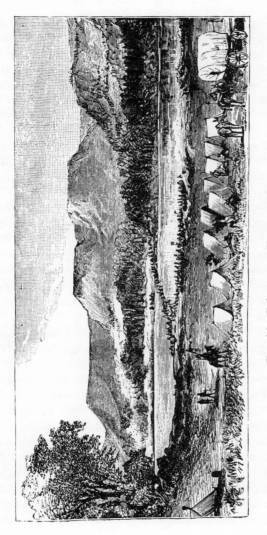

Crook's Column on Tongue River

from surprise; and he and his men hasten off to surrounding hilltops and crests from which they can view the approaches, and at two P.M. we proceed to make ourselves comfortable. We have no huts and only one blanket apiece, but who cares? The August sun is bright and cheery; the air is fresh and clear; the smoke rises, mast-like, high in the skies until it meets the upland breeze that, sweeping down from the Big Horn range behind us, has cleared away the pall of smoke our Indian foes had but yesterday hung before our eyes, and left the valley of the Tongue thus far green and undefiled. We have come but twenty miles, are fresh and vigorous; but the advance reports no signs yet, and Crook halts us so that we may have an early start tomorrow.

We smoke our pipes and doze through the afternoon, stretched at length under the shady trees, and at evening stroll around among the campfires, calling on brother officers of other regiments whom we haven't met before in years. But early enough we roll ourselves in our blankets, and, with heads pillowed on turf or saddle, sleep undisturbed till dawn.

August 6th breaks clear and cloudless. Long before the sun can peer in upon us in our deep nook in the valley, we have had our dip in the cold stream and our steaming and hugely relished breakfast, stowed our tinnikins and pannikins on the pack mules, and wait expectant of "Boots and Saddles!" Again the infantry lead the way, and not until seven do we hear the welcome "Mount!" and follow in their tracks. By this time the sun is pouring down upon us; by nine his rays are scorching, and the dust rises in clouds from the crowded trail. The gorge grows deeper and deeper, the bluffs bolder and more precipitous; we can see nothing but precipice on either side, and, lashed and tormented, the Deje Agie winds a tortuous course between. We cross it

66

again and again—each time it grows deeper and stronger. The trail is so crooked we never see more than a quarter of a mile ahead. At noon we overtake the infantry, phlegmatically stripping off shoes, stockings, and all garments "below the belt," for the eleventh time since they left camp, preparatory to another plunge through the stream; and a tall, red-headed Irishman starts a laugh with his quizzical "Fellers, did e'er a one of yez iver cross on a bridge?"

At two o'clock, after the thirteenth crossing since seven A.M., we again receive orders to halt, unsaddle, and bivouac. Captain Leib and Company "M" mount guard, and with twenty-two miles more to our credit, and with the thick smoke of forest fires drifting overhead, we repeat the performance of yesterday afternoon and night, and wonder when we are to see those Indians.

Reveille and the dawn of the seventh come together. We wake stiff and cold in the keen morning air, but thaw out rapidly under the genial influence of the huge tins of coffee promptly supplied. At six we descry the infantry and the pack trains clambering up the heights to the northwest and disappearing from view over the timbered crests. At seven we again mount and ride down stream a few hundred yards, then turn sharp to the left and up a broad winding ravine along a beaten trail—buffalo and Indian, of great antiquity. Mile after mile we push along up grade—we of the Fifth well to the front today and in view of the scouts and advance most of the time. The woods are thick along the slopes, the grass that was rich and abundant in the valley of the Tongue is becoming sparse. Up we go—the ascent seems interminable. Once in a while we catch glimpses of smoke masses overhead and drifting across the face of distant ridges. At last we see knots of horsemen gathering on a high ridge a mile in front; half an hour's active climbing, mostly afoot and leading our horses, brings us close under them. "Halt" is sounded, and General Carr and I go up to join the party on the crest.

We pause on the very summit of the great divide between the Tongue and the Rosebud, and far to south, north, and west the tumbling sea of ravine and upland, valleys that dip out of sight, mountains that are lost in fleecy clouds, all are spread before us. The view is glorious. We look right down into the cañon of the Rosebud, yet it must be six to eight miles away, and how far down we cannot judge. From every valley north and west rolling clouds of smoke rise towards and blacken the heavens. Somewhere over on those opposite bluffs General Crook had his big fight with the Sioux on the 17 of June, but not a Sioux is in sight.

It takes us three good hours to get down into the valley, and here we receive in grim silence the orders to go into bivouac parallel to the stream, facing west. The Indians have burned off every blade of grass their ponies left undevoured along the narrow gorge, and for miles below us the scouts report it even worse. "The whole Sioux nation has been in camp hereabouts not two weeks ago," says one rugged frontiersman, "and I've been nigh onto ten mile down stream and didn't reach the end of the village." The ground is strewn with abandoned lodgepoles, and covered with relics of Indian occupancy too unmistakable to be pleasant.

The Third and Second Cavalry file into position on the eastern bank parallel with our line, and all the pickets go out at once—Captain Hayes, with Company "G," covering our front.

The situation is romantic, but disagreeable. Some of us sleep rather restlessly that night, and one and all welcome the dawn of the 8th. It is more than chilly in the keen morning air, but we march northward in a thick, smoky haze that utterly obscures the landscape. We can see but a short fifty yards in any direction, and the deeper we ride into it the thicker and more suffocating it becomes. Four or five miles downstream, still riding through the lately occupied camps, we bump up against the rear of the column ahead. An aide leads us off to the left, and informs General Carr that there is good grazing in some little breaks and ravines—to unsaddle and give the horses a chance while we wait for reports from the scouts. Here we "loaf" through the entire day, when suddenly the signal to saddle and mount startles us at six P.M., just as we were thinking of going to sleep. We march very rapidly, six, seven, ten miles, and then darkness sets in. Thicker darkness I never encountered. Men pull out their pipes and whiff away at them till the glow of their sparks looks like a long trail of tiny furnace fires, and gives us a clue to follow. No one but an Indian who has lived among these valleys all his life can be guiding us tonight. At nine o'clock the men are singing darky melodies and Irish songs; and it is not until 10:30 that we file past bivouac fires lighted in a deep bend of the stream, grope our way out to an invisible front, and, fairly hobbling and half-lariating our horses, throw ourselves down by them to sleep. Captain Rodgers is notified that he and Company "A" are "for guard"; and, for a man who cannot or will not swear, Rodgers manages to express his disgust appropriately.

A slight sprinkling of rain comes on at daybreak, and we see the infantry hurrying off northward through the misty light. We soon follow down the right bank, the Fifth Cavalry leading the column of horse. Stanton tells us that a large body of Sioux are not more than four days ahead— were here in force not four days ago. It is easy to see that we are on the trail of an immense number of Indians—eight to ten thousand—but we judge it to be a fortnight old. At 9:15 a cold, driving rain sets in and whirls in our faces as we march. At two P.M. we bivouac again, and begin to growl at this will-o'-the wisp business. The night, for August, is bitter cold. Ice forms on the shallow pools close to shore, and Captain Adam, who commands the guard, declares that the thermometer was at zero at daybreak. "What thermometer?" is the question. "Vell, any thermometer as was tam fool enough to get here—*un'stand?*" is our veteran's characteristic reply, and it puts us in better humor. Stiff and cold when we march at seven o'clock on the 10th, we have not long to suffer from that cause. A bright sun pours down in recompense. We march five miles, halt, and graze awhile; then push on again along a broad, beaten trail over which countless hordes of ponies must have recently passed. Thick clouds of dust rise high above the bluffs on either side; the valley opens out wide and rolling east and west. Here the Indian flight has been so rapid that the work of destruction is incomplete, and the grass is excellent in many a spot. "The grandest country in the world for Indian and buffalo now," says General Carr. "Two years hence it will be the grandest place for cattle."

We of the Fifth are marching down the left or western bank of the Rosebud today, somewhat independently as regards the rest of the cavalry brigade, which, following the infantry, is away across the valley, close under the slopes and hillsides towards the east. About nine in the morning, while I am profiting by a ten-minute halt to jot in my notebook some of the surrounding topographical features, my orderly and myself climb to the top of the ridge on our left from which a good view of the country is to be had. Just here the valley runs northeast, and we have been pursuing that general direction for the last day's march; but right

70

ahead, some two thousand yards, a tall bluff juts out into the valley from the west. The river sweeps round its base in a broad fringe of cottonwoods, and disappears from sight for six or eight miles; then, over an intervening range, I see it again, away to the north, making straight for what must be the valley of the Yellowstone. Between that great bend of the river and the distant bluffs on the eastern side, a broad plain, scorched and blistered by sun and Indian fire, stretches away some two or three miles in width. This side of the bend the slopes gradually near the stream, and the picture below me is a very pretty one. Right under our ridge the Fifth Cavalry, in long column, is just preparing to remount and move on. A mile away to the eastward are our brethren of the Second and Third; a quarter of a mile ahead of them, the compact battalion of infantry. Here and there groups of horses, men, and a fluttering flag indicate the positions in march of Generals Crook and Merritt. Half a mile in advance·of all, those little dots of horsemen are our scouts, while, anyhow and everywhere, in no order whatsoever, our Crows and Shoshones are scattered along the column on one flank, while the pack mules kick up a thick dust on the other. The cloud of dust, in fact, rises from the whole column, and extends way back up the Rosebud; and even as I am wondering how far it can be seen, my eye is attracted by just as thick a cloud around the point, apparently coming up the valley. What the mischief can that be?

Answering our eager signals, General Carr comes hurriedly up the slope and levels his glass. It is dust, sure enough, and lots of it. Nothing but an immense concourse of four-footed animals could raise such a cloud. "Forward!" is the order; "Indians or buffalo?" is the query. "Ride over and report it to General Merritt," says my colonel to me. So "Donnybrook" strikes a rapid lope, and we pick our way through the cottonwoods, over the stream and up the low bank on the other side, where the first thing that meets my eyes is a grand hullabaloo among the Indians, our allies. They are whooping and yelling, throwing blankets and superfluous clothing to the ground—stripping for a fight, evidently—and darting to and fro in wild excitement. Beyond them the troops are massing in close column behind some low bluffs, and, looking back, I see the Fifth coming rapidly through the stream to join them. Evidently my news is no news to General Merritt; but the message is delivered all the same, and I get permission to gallop ahead towards the scouts and see what's coming. I make for a bluff just on the edge of the plain I have described, and, nearing it, can see farther and farther around the great bend. Our scouts and Indians are dashing around in circles, and cautiously approaching the turn. Another minute and I have reached the bluff, and there get a grand view of the coming host. Indians! I should say so—scores of them, darting about in equal excitement to our own. But no Indians are they who keep in close column along that fringe of trees; no Indians are they whose compact squadrons are moving diagonally out across the broad plain, taking equal intervals, then coming squarely towards us at a rapid trot. Then look! Each company, as it comes forward, opens out like the fan of practised coquette, and a sheaf of skirmishers is launched to the front. Something in the snap and style of the whole movement stamps them at once. There is no need of fluttering guidon and stirring trumpet call to identify them; I know the Seventh Cavalry at a glance, and swing my old campaign hat in delighted welcome. Behind them are the solid regiments of Miles and Gibbon, and long trains of wagons and supplies. It is General Terry and his whole array, and our chiefs ride forward to greet them. And then it is that the question is asked, in comical perplexity, "Why, where on earth are the Indians?" Except our allies, none are in sight. They have slipped away between us.

SEVEN

AWAY TO THE YELLOWSTONE

NEVER BEFORE, and never since, has the valley of the Rosebud beheld such a gathering as was there to be seen on that brilliant 10th of August, 1876—brilliant, that is to say, as nature could make it, for in General Crook's command, at least, there was nothing of embellishment. The war of the Revolution, the huts of Valley Forge, never exhibited so sombre an array of soldiery as we presented when General Terry and his brigade confronted us at the great bend.

It may be said that we were surprised at the meeting, and it can be established that they were astonished. Marching up the valley, General Terry was in daily expectation of finding a mass of Indians in his front. At latest accounts they were in strong force—in thousands, no doubt—between him and General Crook's position at the base of the Big Horn, and he commenced his aggressive move with every precaution, and with supplies for a long and stirring campaign. He had with him a complete wagon train, tents and equipage of every description. We had a few days' bacon and hardtack, coffee and sugar, and a whole arsenal of ammunition on our mules, but not a tent, and only one blanket apiece. He had artillery in the shape of a few light fieldpieces and was making slow, cautious advances up the Rosebud at the rate of eight or ten miles a day. He had not come upon a single recent Indian "sign," yet knew that the country to the south must have been full of them within the fortnight. So when his scouts reported an immense cloud of dust coming down the valley above the bend, and his Indian allies began the same absurd gyrations and uproar which we had observed in ours, he very naturally supposed that a horde of hostiles was sweeping down to the attack, and made his dispositions accordingly.

It was my good fortune to be in our advance and to witness the beautiful deployment of the Seventh Cavalry over the plains in our front, and it is hard to say which side would have whipped if we had not discovered that neither was Sioux. A report gained credence later in the day that Dr. Clements, Crook's medical director, said that it would be Sioux-icidal to fight under the circumstances; but his friends believed that this eruptiveness was due to professional disappointment at the nonemployment of himself and his able assistants, and the matter was hushed up.

Pending the solution of the problem as to the whereabouts of our common foe, the two brigades were ordered to camp at once, and make themselves at home. The generals met and discussed the situation, the scouts made hurried examination of the surrounding country, and the mystery was at an end. Leaving the valley of the Rosebud at the very point where our two commands had confronted each other on the 10th, a broad trail of recent date led away eastward over the divide towards Tongue River. The low hills were stamped into dust by the hoofs of countless ponies. Sitting Bull, Crazy Horse, Spotted Eagle and the hosts of different kinds of wolves and bears and cultures in which their savage nomenclature rejoices, had fairly given us the slip, and probably ten thousand Indians of various ages and both sexes had swarmed across Terry's long front on the Yellowstone, but beyond the range of his scouts.

75

That a large portion of them would attempt to cross the great rivers farther to the east and escape towards the Canada line was instantly divined, and a prompt man was needed to head a rush back to and then down the Yellowstone to hold the stream and its crossings and check the Indian flight, while our main body pursued along the trail. In less than an hour General Miles had gone to the right about with his regiment and the light guns and was making long strides towards the north. The world has since read of the tireless energy with which this vigorous soldier has continued the work he commenced that day. Winter and summer, from one end of the Yellowstone Valley to the other, he has persistently and most successfully hunted the hostiles, until his name has become a synonym for dash and good luck. Two of his companies had been stationed with us all the previous winter at Fort Riley, in Kansas, and I was eager to get over to their camp to see them as soon as my duties were through; but long before our horses were herded out on the foothills, and I had seen Captain Montgomery and Company "B" posted as our guards, a new column of dust was rising down the valley, and our Fifth Infantry friends were gone.

The afternoon and evening were spent by the officers of the two commands in pleasant reunion. We had nowhere to "receive" and no refreshments to offer; so by tacit agreement, Terry's people became the hosts, we the guests, and it was fun to mark the contrast in our appearance. General Terry, as became a brigadier, was attired in the handsome uniform of his rank; his staff and his line officers, though looking eminently serviceable, were all in neat regimentals, so that shoulder straps were to be seen in every direction. General Crook, as became an old campaigner and frontiersman, was in a rough hunting rig, and in all his staff and line there was not a complete suit of uniform. Left to our fancy in the matter, we had fallen back upon our comfortable old Arizona scouting suits, and were attired in deerskin, buckskin, flannels, and corduroy; but in the Fifth Cavalry, you could not have told officer from private. It may have been suitable as regarded Indian campaigning, but was undeniably slouchy and border-ruffianish. It needed some persuasion to induce old and intimate friends to believe in our identity; and General Terry's engineer officer and his commissary, who had been chosen "chums" of mine in West Point days, roared with laughter at the metamorphosis.

Their tents were brightly lighted and comfortably furnished. Even the Seventh Cavalry were housed like Sybarites to our unaccustomed eyes. "Great guns!" said our new major, almost exploding at a revelation so preposterous. "Look at Reno's tent—he's got a Brussels carpet!" But they made us cordially welcome and were civilly unconscious of our motley attire.

While the chieftains and their staffs discussed the plans for the morrow, we unresponsible juniors contentedly accepted the situation, but by nine P.M. it was known that at early dawn we of Crook's command were to reload our pack mules with rations from Terry's wagons and continue the pursuit. Now it began to dawn upon us that we had seen the last of our comforts—our wagons, tents, beds, and clothing—for an indefinite period; and in Indian warfare particularly, is a stern chase a long chase—unless you have the lead at start.

That night we were bivouacked in the thick underbrush along the Rosebud, hugging the tortuous bends of the stream, and as much as possible keeping our herds between our lines and the river. Suddenly the stillness was broken by a snort of terror among the horses; then a rush as of a mighty whirlwind, the crash of a thousand hoofs, a shot or two, and the shouts of excited men, and the herds of Companies "A," "B," and "M" disappeared in a twinkling. Seized by some sudden and unaccountable panic, they had snapped their "side lines" like packthread, torn their picket pins from the loose, powdery soil, and with one wild dash had cleared the company lines, and, tracked by the dying thunder of their hoofs, were fleeing for dear life far to the westward. Officers and men sprang to arms, anticipating attack from Indians. Many of the First Battalion had been trampled and bruised in the stampede; but in a moment a dozen experienced campaigners were in saddle and off in pursuit, and towards morning, after miles of hard riding, the runaways were skilfully "herded" back to camp. But the night's adventure cost us the services of one of our very best officers, as Lieutenant Eaton's pistol was accidentally discharged in the rush, and tore off a portion of the index finger of his right hand.

The following morning, August 11th, was by General Crook's people, at least, spent in drawing rations from the wagons of Terry's command. At ten o'clock our pack mules were again loaded up, and by eleven the Fifth Cavalry were filing eastwardly out of the valley; marched rapidly on the Indian trail, found the valley of the Tongue River only nine miles away across a picturesque divide, descended into a thickly timbered bottom, marched only a couple of miles downstream, and there received orders to halt, bivouac again, and were told to wait for Terry's command to join us. We moved into a dense grove of timber—lofty and corpulent old cottonwoods. Company "D" (Sumner's) posted its guards and pickets, and the rest of us became interested in the great quantity of Indian pictures and hieroglyphics on the trees. We were camping on a favorite "stamping ground" of theirs, evidently, for the trees were barked in every direction for some distance from the ground, and covered with specimens of aboriginal art. Sketches of warriors scalping soldiers, carrying off women on horseback, hunting buffalo, etc., but with the perceptible preference for the stirring scenes of soldier fighting. That had become more popular than ever since the Custer massacre. While examining these specimens, I was attracted by a shout and the gathering of a knot of soldiers around some fallen timber. Joining them, and stepping over the low barrier of logs, I came upon the body of a white man, unscalped, who had evidently made a desperate fight for life, as the ground was covered with the shells of his cartridges; but a bullet through the brain had finally laid him low, and his savage foeman had left him as he fell, probably a year before we came upon the spot.

Towards sunset the clouds that had gathered all day, and sprinkled us early in the afternoon, opened their floodgates, and the rain came down in torrents. We built Indian "wickyups" of saplings and elastic twigs, threw ponchos and blankets over them, and crawled under; but 'twas no use. Presently the whole country was flooded, and we built huge fires, huddled around them in the squashy mud, and envied our horses, who really seemed pleased at the change. General Terry and his cavalry and infantry marched past our bivouac early in the evening, went on downstream, and camped somewhere among the timber below. We got through the night, I don't remember how, exactly; and my notebook is not very full of details of this and the next four days. We would have been wetter still on the following morning—Saturday, the 12th—if we *could* have been, for it rained too hard to march, and we hugged our campfires until one P.M., when it gave signs of letting up a little and we saddled and marched away down the Tongue ten or eleven miles, by which time it was nearly dark, raining harder than ever. General Carr and Mr. Barbour Lathrop (the correspondent of the San Francisco *Call,* who had turned out to be an old acquaintance of some older friends of mine, and whose vivacity was unquenchable, even by such weather as this) made a double wickyup under the only tree there was on the open plain on which we camped for the night, and, seeing what looked to be a little bunch of timber through the mist a few hundred yards away, I went to prospect for a lodging; found it to be one of the numerous aërial sepulchres of the Sioux, which we had been passing for the last four days—evidences that Custer's dying fight was not so utterly one-sided, after all. But, unattractive as this was for a mortal dwelling place, its partial shelter was already pre-empted, and, like hundreds of others, I made an open night of it.

Sunday morning we pushed on again, wet and bedraggled. No hope of catching the Sioux now, but we couldn't turn back. The valley was filled with the parallel columns—Crook's and Terry's—cavalry and infantry marching side by side. We made frequent halts in the mud and rain; and during one of these I had a few moments' pleasant chat with General Gibbon, who, as usual, had a host of reminiscences of the grand old Iron Brigade to speak of, and many questions to ask of his Wisconsin comrades. It was the one bright feature of an otherwise dismal day. At 4:30 P.M. the columns are halted for the night, and the cavalry lose not a moment in hunting grass for their horses. Fortunately it is abundant here and of excellent quality, and this adds force to the argument that the Indians must have scattered. The scouts still prate of big trails ahead; but our horses are becoming weak for want of grain, our Indian allies are holding big powwows every evening, the Crows still talk war and extermination to the Sioux, but the Shoshones have never been so far away from home in their lives, and begin to weaken. Several of them urge additional reasons indicative of the fact that the ladies of the tribe are not regarded by their lords as above suspicion in times of such prolonged absence. That evening Captains Weir and McDougall of the Seventh Cavalry spent an hour or so at our fire and gave us a detailed account of their fight on the 25th, on the Little Big Horn. They were with Reno on the bluffs, and had no definite knowledge of the fate of Custer and his five companies until high noon on the 27th, when relieved by General Gibbon. Then they rode at once to the field, and came upon the remains of their comrades.

"It must have been a terrible sensation when you first caught sight of them," said one of their listeners.

"Well, no," replied McDougall. "In fact, the first thought that seemed to strike every man of us, and the first words spoken were, 'How white they look!' We knew what to expect, of course; and they had lain there stripped for nearly forty-eight hours."

That night the rain continued, and at daybreak on the 14th the Fifth Cavalry got up and spent an hour or so in vain attempts at wringing the wet from blanket and over-coat. By 7:15 we all moved northward again, though I could see scouts far out on the low hills on our right flank. For half an hour we of the Fifth marched side by side with the Seventh, and our gaunt horses and ragged-looking riders made but a poor appearance in such society. Nearing a ford of the Tongue River, we found some little crowding and confusion. The heads of columns were approaching the same point upon the bank, and we were just about hunting for a new ford when the Seventh Cavalry made a rapid oblique,

81

and Major Reno doffed his straw hat to General Carr, with the intimation that we had the "right of way"—a piece of courtesy which our commander did not fail to acknowledge.

Another ford, from the left bank this time, and before us, coming in from the east, is a valley bounded by low, rolling hills for a few miles, but farther to the eastward we note that high bulwarks of rock are thrown up against the sky. Into this valley we turn; the grass is good, the water is all too plentiful; occasional fallen trees in the stream promise fuel in abundance; but we look somewhat wistfully down the Tongue, for not more than fifteen miles away rolls the Yellowstone. And now once more, as the rain comes down in torrents, we unsaddle, turn our horses out to graze, Kellogg and Company "I" are posted as guards, and we wonder what is going to be done. Only noon, and only ten miles have we come from last camp. Colonel Royall marches his "brigade" farther upstream and follows our example, and then comes over to exchange commiserations with General Carr. The veterans are neither of them in best possible humor. A story is going the rounds about Royall that does us all good, even in that dismal weather. A day or two before, so it was told, Royall ordered one of his battalion commanders to "put that battalion in camp on the other side of the river, facing east." A prominent and well-known characteristic of the subordinate officer referred to was a tendency to split hairs, discuss orders, and, in fine, to make trouble where there was a ghost of a chance of so doing unpunished. Presently the Colonel saw that his instructions were not being carried out, and, not being in a mood for indirect action, he put spurs to his horse, dashed through the stream, and reined up alongside the victim with, "Didn't I order you, sir, to put your battalion in camp along the river—facing east?"

"Yes, sir; but this ain't a river. It's only a creek."

"Creek be d——d, sir! It's a river—a river from this time forth, *by order,* sir. Now do as I tell you."

There was no further delay.

All that day and night we lay along Pumpkin Creek. "Squashy Creek" was suggested as a name at once more descriptive and appropriate. The soil was like sponge from the continuous rain. At daybreak it was still raining, and we mounted and rode away eastward—Terry and Crook, cavalry and infantry, pack mules and all, over an unmistakable Indian trail that soon left the Pumpkin, worked through the "malpais," and carried us finally to the crest of a high, commanding ridge, from which we could see the country in every direction for miles. The rain held up a while—not long enough for us to get dry, but to admit of our looking about and becoming convinced of the desolation of our surroundings. The trail grew narrow and more tortuous, plunged down into a cañon ahead, and as we left the crest I glanced back for a last view of the now distant valley of the Tongue. What it might be in beautiful weather no words of mine would accurately describe, because at such times I have not seen it. What it is in rainy weather no words could describe. And yet it was comfort compared to what was before us.

At noon we were gazing out over the broad valley of Powder River, the Chakadee Wakpa of the Sioux. Below us the Mizpah, flowing from the southwest, made junction with the broader stream, and we, guided by our Indians, forded both above the confluence, and went on down the valley. And so it was for two more days; rain, mud, wet, and cold. Rations were soaked; and we, who had nothing but salt meat and hardtack, began to note symptoms of scurvy among the men. But we were pushing for supplies now.

The Indians had scattered up every valley to the eastward; their pony tracks led in myriads over the prairie slopes east of the Powder. We could go no farther without sustenance of some kind, and so, on the afternoon of Thursday, the 17th, we toiled down to the valley of the Yellowstone and scattered in bivouac along its ugly, muddy banks. The rain ceased for a while, but not a boat was in sight, no news from home, no mail, no supplies—nothing but dirt and discomfort. We could only submit to the inevitable, and wait.

EIGHT

AGAIN ON THE TRAIL

OUR FIRST IMPRESSIONS of the Yellowstone, as seen from the mouth of the Powder River, were dismal in the last degree; but it was an undoubted case of "any port in a storm." General Terry's supply boat put in a prompt appearance and we drew rations again on Friday and received intimations that we might move at any moment. "Which way?" was the not unnatural question, and "Don't know" the laconic yet comprehensive answer.

The rain that had deluged us on the march down the valleys of the Tongue and Powder had ceased from sheer exhaustion, and we strove to dry our overcoats and blankets at the big fires built in the timber. We had signalized our meeting with Terry's command by a royal bonfire which lit up the country by night and poured a huge column of smoke skywards by day; but as it was contrary to orders, and a most vivid indication of our position, Colonel Mason's battalion received a scathing rebuke for carelessness, and Mason was mad enough to follow the lead of the historic Army of Flanders. A most conscientious and faithful officer, it seemed to sting him to the quick that any one of his companies should have been guilty of such recklessness. So the day after we reached the Yellowstone, and the horses of the regiments were all grazing out along the prairie slopes south of camp and revelling in the rich and plentiful buffalo grass, while all officers and men not on guard were resting along the banks of the stream and growling at the vigorous gale that swept down from the north and whirled the sand in one's eyes, there came a sudden shout of fire, and Major Upham and I, who were trying to make a "wickyup" that would exclude the wind, became aware of a column of flame and smoke rolling up in the very centre of his battalion. In a moment it became evident that the biggest kind of a prairie fire was started. The men of Company "I" were hurrying their arms and equipments to the windward side, and as one man the rest of the regiment came running to the scene, swinging their saddle blankets in air.

Fanned by the hurricane blowing at the time, the flames swept over the ground with the force of a blast furnace; tufts of burning grass were driven before the great surging wave of fire, and, falling far out on the prairie became the nuclei of new conflagrations. Fire call was promptly sounded by the chief trumpeter and repeated along the lines. The distant herds were rapidly moved off to right and left and hurried in towards the river. The whole command that was in bivouac west of the Powder River turned out to fight the common enemy; but in ten minutes, in all the might of its furious strength, a grand conflagration was sweeping southward towards the rolling hills, and consuming all before it.

Like the great Chicago fire, it started from a cause trivial enough, but, spreading out right and left, it soon had a front of over half a mile, and not till it had run fully two miles to the south was it finally checked. Captain Hayes and a party of old and experienced hands "raced" it far out to the front, and, there setting fire to the grass, extinguishing it from the south and forcing it back against the wind, they succeeded after much hard work in burning off a number of large areas in front of the advancing wall of flame, fought fire with fire, and in two hours were masters of the situation. But most of our grass was gone; and Saturday afternoon, at four o'clock, we of the Fifth saddled and marched up the Yellowstone in search of fresh pasture. A mile was all we had to go, and moving was no trouble to men who had neither roof nor furniture.

We rode into line in the river bottom again. General Carr, with the headquarters party, seized upon a huge log at least a yard in diameter that lay close to the river brink; and with this as a backbone we built such rude shelter as could be made with leaves, boughs, and a ragged poncho or two, crawled in and made our beds upon the turf. General Merritt and his staff found shelter in a little grove a few yards away, and with the coming of Sunday morning all had enjoyed a good rest.

Meantime we learned that Buffalo Bill had ridden all alone down toward the Glendive, bent on a scout to ascertain if the Indians were attempting to cross the river. I did not envy him the peril of that sixty-mile jaunt through the Bad Lands, but it was an old story to him. We were to remain in camp to await his report. It seemed that nothing definite had been ascertained as to the movements of the Indians; and for five days we rested there on the Yellowstone, nothing of interest transpiring, and nothing of especial pleasure.

General Carr, to keep us from rusting, ordered inspection and mounted drills on Sunday and Monday morning; but then the rain came back, and for forty-eight hours we were fairly afloat. It rained so hard Tuesday and Wednesday nights that the men gave up all idea of sleep, built great fires along the banks, and clustered round them for warmth. Shelter there was none. Some of our officers and men, who had broken down in the severity of the ordeal, were examined by the surgeons, and those who were deemed too sick for service were ordered home on the steamer *Far West,* which would take them by river as far as Bismarck. Among them was Captain Goodloe, of the Twenty-second Infantry, who had been prostrated by a paralytic stroke on the last day's march towards the Yellowstone; and of our own regiment we were forced to part with Lieutenant Eaton, whose severe hurt received the night of the stampede on the Rosebud had proved disabling for campaign work. At this time, too, some of our newspaper correspondents concluded that the chances of a big fight were too small to justify their remaining longer with so unlucky an expedition, and the representative of the San Francisco *Call* and an odd genius who had joined us at Fort Fetterman and speedily won the sobriquet of "Calamity Jim," concluded that their services would be worth more in some other field.

A great loss to us was in Buffalo Bill, whose theatrical engagements demanded his presence in the East early in the fall; and most reluctantly he, too, was compelled to ask his release. He left his "pardner," Jim White, with us to finish the campaign; and we little thought that those two sworn friends were meeting for the last time on earth when "Buffalo Chips" bade good-bye to Buffalo Bill.

Ten soldiers of the Fifth were pronounced incapacitated by the examiners and ordered to return. Among them was an elderly man who had joined the regiment in June with a good character from the Fourth Cavalry. The Custer massacre had so preyed upon his mind as to temporarily destroy his intellect, or make it too keen for the wits of the Medical Department. I believe that up to the last moment it was an open question whether Caniff (for such was his name) was downright insane or only shamming; but he carried his point, and got away from the danger he dreaded. "But, Lord, sir," as the corporal in charge of the detachment afterwards told me, "he was the sensiblest man you ever see by the time we got past Bismarck." In fact, it would look as though that Custer massacre had been responsible for the unmanning of just three members of the Fifth Cavalry; and, to the ineffable disgust of the veteran Company "K," two of them were privates in its ranks.

Our stay of six days on the Yellowstone presented no features of general interest. A brace of trading boats swept down with the current from the markets of the Gallatin Valley, and some of us were able to purchase, at fabulous prices, new suits of underclothing and a quantity of potatoes and onions, of which the men stood sadly in need. More supplies of grain and rations arrived, and our horses had a few nibbles of oats, but not enough to build up any of their lost strength. General Terry, from the east side of the Powder, rode over one day to pay a visit to General Crook; and the story goes that our brigadier was pointed out to him squatted on a rock in the Yellowstone, and with that absorbed manner which was his marked characteristic, and a disregard for "style" never before equalled in the history of one of his rank, scrubbing away at his hunting shirt.

Thursday morning, August the 24th, chilled and soaked, we marched away from the Yellowstone, and mostly on foot, leading our gaunt horses through the thick mud of the slopes along the Powder, we toiled some ten miles; then halted for the night. Then it cleared off, and night came on in cloudless beauty, but sharply cold. Next morning we hung about our fires long after our frugal breakfast, waiting for the signal to saddle and march. Trumpet calls were forbidden "until further orders"; and it was divined that now, at least, we might hope to see the Indians who had led us this exasperating chase. But it was long before we reached them, and this narrative is running threadbare with dry detail. Let me condense from my notebook the route and incidents of the march to Heart River, where we finally gave up the chase:

General Terry's cavalry—Seventh and Second—followed us on the march of the 25th, after we had forded Powder River and started up the eastern bank; camped again that night in the valley after long and muddy march. At seven A.M. on the 26th we of Crook's army cut loose from any base, and marched square to the east; and General Terry, with his entire command, bade us farewell, and hurried back to the Yellowstone. Couriers had reached him during the night with important information, and he and his people were needed along the crossings of the great river while we hunted the redskins over the prairies. The weather was lovely, the country rolling and picturesque; but far and near the Indians had burned away the grass. Camped on the west fork of O'Fallon's Creek. Game abundant all around us, but no firing allowed.

Sunday, 27th.—Marched seven A.M. at rear of column, north of east; rolling country; no timber; little grass; crossed large branch of O'Fallon's Creek at eleven A.M., where some pack mules were stalled, but finally got through. Bivouac one P.M. in dry east fork of same creek.

Monday, 28th.—Day beautiful and cool; march rapid and pleasant along the trail on which Terry and Custer came west in May and June. Country beautifully bold and undulating, with fine grass everywhere. We halted on Cabin Creek at 1:30 P.M.; and two hours after, over in the direction of Beaver Creek to the northeast, two large smokes floated up into the still air. Just at sunset there came on a thunderstorm, with rain, hail, and vivid lightning—hailstones as big as acorns, and so plentifully pelting that with great difficulty we restrained our horses from stampede. The lightning kindled the prairie just in front of the pickets, and the rain came only in time to save our grass. Of course, we were drenched with rain and hammered with hail.

Tuesday, 29th.—Most beautiful day's march yet; morning lovely after the storm. We move rapidly on trail of the infantry, and at ten o'clock are astonished at seeing them massing in close column by division on the southwest side of grassy slopes that loom up to a great height, and were soon climbing the bluffs beyond them—an ascent of some five to six hundred feet.

Here General Merritt gave the regiment a lesson which it richly deserved. Fuel had been a little scarce on one or two recent occasions; and some of the men, finding a few logs at the foot of the bluffs, hoisted them on their tottering horses, and were clambering in this fashion up the ascent, when the "Chief" caught sight of them. The General is a man of great restraint at such a time, but, without the employment of language either profane or profuse, he managed to convey an intimation to some eighty acres of hillside, in less than five seconds, that those logs should be dropped; and they were. Later in the day he devoted a half-hour to the composition of a general order expressive at once of his views on the matter which had excited his wrath in the morning, and his intentions with reference to

91

future offenders. Winding up, as it did, with a scathing denunciation of this "violation of the first principles" of a cavalryman's creed, we of the Fifth felt sore for a week after; but it served us right, and the offence did not occur again.

We found ourselves on the crest of a magnificent range, from which we looked down into the beautiful valley of the Beaver to the east, and southward over mile after mile of sharp, conical buttes that were utterly unlike anything we had seen before. We had abundant water and grass, and here we rested two days, while our scouts felt their way out towards the Little Missouri.

Thursday, the 31st, with a cold norther blowing, we went down the Beaver ten miles to the north, halted and conducted the bi-monthly muster demanded by the regulations, and again the scouts swept over the country in vain search of Indian signs, while we waited until late the following afternoon for their reports, and then merely moved down the valley another eight miles for the night. On the 2d we put in a good day's work, marching rapidly and steadily until two P.M., still in the beautiful wild valley of the Beaver, catching glimpses during the day of the tall Sentinel Buttes off to our right. Next day we turned square to the east again, jogging quickly along through hills and upland that grew bolder and higher every hour; camped at head of Andrew's Creek; pushed on again on the following morning (Monday, September 4th), cold and shivering in another norther —by nine the rain pouring in torrents. As we neared the Little Missouri the hills became higher, outcroppings of coal were to be seen along every mile. Finally, we debouched through a long, deep, tortuous cañon into the Little Missouri itself, forded and bivouacked in a fine grove of timber, where, the rain having ceased again, and with fine, blazing fires in every direction, we spent a night of comfort.

The Indians must be near at hand. The timber, the valley, the fords and crossings, all indicate their recent presence. Tomorrow's sun should bring them before our eyes. At daybreak we are up and ready. The day is drizzly, and the command don't seem to care a pin by this time. We are becoming amphibious, and so long as the old cavalryman has a quid of good tobacco to stow in his taciturn jaws he will jog along contentedly for hours, though the rain descend in cataracts.

Our march leads us southeastward up the valley of Davis's Creek—a valley that grows grandly beautiful as we near its head. We of the Fifth are some distance from the head of column as we climb out upon the fine plateau that here stretches for miles from the head of the creek towards the streams that rise a day's march away and flow towards the Missouri. Away in front we can see General Crook and his staff; far out beyond them are tiny dots of horsemen, whom we know to be Stanton and the scouts. Every now and then a deer darts into sight along the column, and now permission is given to shoot; for we are over a hundred miles from the nearest chance for supplies, and have only two days' rations left. We are following those Indians to the bitter end.

Suddenly, away to the front, rapid shots are heard. A moment they sound but a mile distant; in another moment they are dying out of hearing. We prick up our ears and gather reins. Looking back, I see the long column of bearded faces lighting up in eager expectation, but no order comes to hasten our advance. We hear later that our scouts had succeeded in getting near enough to exchange shots with a small war party of Sioux; but their ponies were fresh and fleet, our horses weak and jaded, and there was no possibility of catching them.

Late that afternoon we halt at the head of Heart River. And now at last it looks as though we are whipped without a fight. We not only have not caught the Indians, but we have run out of rations. Only forty-eight hours' full supplies are left, but a little recent economizing has helped us to a spare day or so on half-rations. It is hard for us, but hardest of all for the General, and it is plain that he is deeply disappointed. But action is required, and at once. We can easily make Fort Abraham Lincoln in four days; but, by doing so, we leave all the great stretch of country to the south open to the hostiles, and the Black Hills settlements defenceless. Just how long it will take us to march to Deadwood cannot be predicted. It is due south by compass, but over an unknown country. While the Chief is deciding, we lie down in the cold and wet and try to make ourselves comfortable. Those who are tired of the campaign and hungry for a dinner predict that the morning will find us striking for the Missouri posts; but those who have served long with General Crook, and believe that there is a hostile Indian between us and the Black Hills, roll into their blankets with the conviction that we will have a fight out of this thing yet.

Many a horse has given out already, and dismounted men are plodding along by the flank of column. We have been on half-rations for three days, and are not a little ravenous in consequence, and our campaign suits, which were shabby on the Rosebud, are rags and tatters now. As Colonel Mason and I are "clubbing" our ponchos and blankets for the night, I turn to my old captain, with whom it has been my good fortune to serve so long and still not to lose him on his promotion, and ask, "Well, what do you think of it?" And Mason, who is an inveterate old growler around garrison in the piping times of peace, and stanchest and most loyal of subordinates in trying times in the field, answers as I could have predicted: "We oughtn't to give up yet, on account of a little roughing it; and *Crook's not the man to do it.*"

NINE

THE FIGHT OF THE REAR GUARD

RAGGED AND ALMOST STARVING, out of rations, out at elbows and every other exposed angle, out of everything but pluck and ammunition, General Crook gave up the pursuit of Sitting Bull at the head of Heart River. The Indians had scattered in every direction. We had chased them a month, and were no nearer than when we started. Their trail led in as many different directions as there are degrees in the circle; they had burned off the grass from the Yellowstone to the mountains, and our horses were dropping by scores, starved and exhausted, every day we marched. There was no help for it, and only one thing left to do. At daybreak the next morning the orders came, "Make for the Black Hills —due south by compass—seven days' march at least," and we headed our dejected steeds accordingly and shambled off in search of supplies.

Through eleven days of pouring, pitiless rain we plodded on that never-to-be-forgotten trip, and when at last we sighted Bare Butte and halted, exhausted, at the swift-flowing current of the Belle Fourche, three-fourths of our cavalry, of the Second, Third, and Fifth regiments, had made the last day's march afoot. One-half our horses were broken down for good, one-fourth had fallen never to rise again, and dozens had been eaten to keep us, their riders, alive.

Enlivening incidents were few enough, and—except one

—of little interest to Milwaukeeans. That one is at your service. On the night of September 7th we were halted near the headwaters of Grand River. Here a force of one hundred and fifty men of the Third Cavalry, with the serviceable horses of that regiment, were pushed ahead under Major Anson Mills, with orders to find the Black Hills, buy up all the supplies he could in Deadwood, and then hurry back to meet us. Two days after, just as we were breaking up our cheerless bivouac of the night, a courier rode in with news that Mills was surrounded by the Indians twenty miles south, and every officer and man of the Fifth Cavalry whose horse had strength enough to trot pushed ahead to the rescue. Through mud, mist, and rain we plunged along, and by half-past ten were exchanging congratulations with Mills and shots with the redskins in as wealthy an Indian village, for its size, as ever we had seen. Custer's guidons and uniforms were the first things that met our eyes—trophies and evidence at once of the part our foe had taken in the bloody battle of the Little Big Horn. Mills had stumbled upon the village before day, made a magnificent dash, and scattered the Indians to the neighboring heights, Slim Buttes by name, and then hung on to his prize like a bulldog, and in the face of appalling odds, till we rode in to his assistance. That afternoon, reinforced by swarms of warriors, they made a grand rally and spirited attack, but 'twas no use. By that time we had some two thousand to meet them, and the whole Sioux nation couldn't have whipped us. Some four hundred ponies had been captured with the village, and many a fire was lighted and many a suffering stomach gladdened with a welcome change from horse meat, tough and stringy, to rib roasts of pony, grass-fed, sweet, and succulent. There is no such sauce as starvation.

Next morning, at break of day, General Crook, with the

wounded, the Indian prisoners, his sturdy infantry, and all the cavalry but one battalion of the Fifth Regiment, pushed on for the south through the same overhanging pall of dripping mist. They had to go. There wasn't a hard-tack north of Deadwood, and men must eat to live.

The First Battalion of the Fifth he left to burn completely the village with all its robes, furs, and Indian treasures, and to cover the retreat.

As the last of the main column disappeared through the drizzle, with Mason's skirmishers thrown well out upon their right flank, a light wind swept upward the veil of smoke and mist, and the panorama became evident to us and to the surrounding Indians at one and the same moment. There was no time to take observations—down they came with a rush.

On a little knoll in the centre of the burning village a group of horsemen has halted—General Carr, who commands the Fifth Cavalry, his staff and orderlies—and the first remark as the fog raises falls from the lips of the Adjutant: "By Jove! Here's a Badger State benefit!"

All along the line the attack has commenced and the battalion is sharply engaged—fighting afoot, their horses being already led away after the main column, but within easy call. Our orders are to follow, but to stand off the Indians. They are not wanted to accompany the march. It is one thing "to stand off the Indians" and hold your ground —it is quite another to stand him off and fall back. They are dashing about on their nimble ponies, following up the line as it doggedly retires from ridge to ridge, far outnumbering us, and all the time keeping up a rattling fire and a volley of aboriginal remarks at our expense. "Lo" yells with unaffected glee when his foe falls back, and it sometimes sounds not unlike the "y-i-i-i-ip" of the rebels in '63. Along our line there is a businesslike taciturnity, an occasional brief, ringing word of command from some officer, or a half-repressed chuckle of delight as some Patlander sees an Indian reel in his saddle, and turns to mutter to his neighbor on the skirmish line that he'd "softened the wax in that boy's ears." Occasionally, too, some man suddenly drops carbine, claps his hand to leg, arm, or side, and with an odd mixture of perplexity and pain in his face looks appealingly to the nearest officer. Our surgeon is just bandaging a bullet hole for one such, but finds time to look up and ask:

"Why Badger State benefit, King? I don't see the point?"

"Just because there are six Wisconsin men right here on this slope," is the answer, "and dozens more for aught I know."

Look at them if you will. I warrant no resident of the Cream City could recognize his townsmen today. Remember, we've been hunting Sioux and Cheyennes since May; haven't seen a shanty for three months, or a tent for two; haven't had a change of raiment for eight weeks, or a shave for ten; and, under those battered slouch hats and in that tattered dress, small wonder that you fail to know the wearers. Right in our front, halfway to the skirmish line, rides the Major commanding the battalion; a tall, solidly-built fellow, with twinkling blue eyes and a bronzed face, barely visible under the mass of blond hair and beard over which the rain is dripping. He is a Milwaukeean and a West Pointer, a stanch favorite, too; and today the whole rear guard is his command, and on his shoulders rests the safety of our move. His is an ugly, trying duty, but he meets it well. Just now he is keenly watching the left of his line, and by a trick he has of hitching forward in his saddle when things don't go exactly right, you see that something's coming. A quick gesture calls up a young officer who is carelessly lounging on a rawboned sorrel that sniffs excitedly at the puffs of smoke floating past his nose. Quick as the gesture the officer straightens in his saddle, shifts a quid into his "off" cheek, and reins up beside his commander. The Major points to the left and front, and away goes the subaltern at a sputtering gallop. Milwaukee is sending Fond du Lac to make the left company "come down out of that." They have halted on a rocky ridge from which they can gloriously pepper the would-be pursuers, and they don't want to quit. The major is John J. Upham, the subaltern is Lieutenant H. S. Bishop.

Square in front, striding down the opposite slope and up towards us come the Company "G" skirmishers. A minute more and the ridge they have left is swarming with Indians. "Halt!" rings out along the line, and quick as thought the troopers face about, fling themselves *ventre à terre* and blaze away, scattering the Sioux like chaff.

There's a stalwart, bearded fellow commanding the right skirmishers of the company, steadily noting the fire of his men. Never bending himself, he moves from point to point cautioning such "new hands" as are excitedly throwing away their shots. He is their first sergeant, a crack soldier; Milwaukee, too—for in old days at Engelmann's school we knew him as Johnny Goll. Listen to his captain, half a head taller and quite as prominent and persistent a target, who is shaking a gauntleted fist at his subordinate and shouting, "I've told you to keep down a dozen times, Sergeant; now, by God, I want you to do it." This makes the nearest men grin. The others are too busy to hear it.

The scene is picturesque enough from our point of view. To the south, two miles away by this time, Crook's long column is crawling snakelike over the rolling sward. To the west the white crags and boulders of the buttes shut off

100

the view—we are fighting along at their very base. Northward the country rises and falls in alternate grassy ridge and ravine; not a tree in sight—only the low-hanging pall of smoke from the burning village in the near distance; the slopes swarming with dusky horsemen, dashing towards us, whooping, yelling, firing, and retiring, always at speed, except where some practised marksman springs from his pony and prone upon the ground draws bead at our chiefs. Between their restless ranks and us is only the long, thin line of cavalry skirmishers, slowly falling back face to the foe, and giving them gun for gun. Eastward, as far as the eye can reach, the country rolls away in billowy undulations, and—look! There comes a dash of Indians around our right flank. See them sweeping along that ridge? Upham is on low ground at this moment and they are beyond his view, but General Carr sees the attempt to cut us off, and in a second the adjutant of the regiment comes tearing to the line, fast as jaded horse can carry him. A comprehensive gesture accomplishes at once the soldierly salute to the Major and points out the new danger. Kellogg's company swings into saddle and fairly springs to the right to meet it.

In buckskin trousers, fringed and beaded, but much the worse for wear, in ragged old hunting shirt and shapeless hat, none but the initiated would recognize Milwaukee, much less West Point, in that adjutant. But he was marker of our Light Guard years before the war, and the first member of its corps of drummer boys. He is just speeding a grim-looking cavalryman, one of the headquarters orderlies, off with a despatch to General Merritt, and that orderly is a Milwaukeean, too, and may have to "run the gauntlet" getting that message through; but his face, what you can see of it through grizzled hair and beard, looks unconcerned enough; and under the weather-stained exterior he is known

101

to be a faithful old soldier—one who loves the rough life better than he did the desk in ante bellum days when he was clerking at Hathaway & Belden's. "Old George," as the men call him, ran a train on the Watertown road, too, once upon a time; but about the close of the war he drifted from the volunteers into the regulars, and there he has stuck ever since.

But all this time Crook is marching away faster than we can back and follow him. We have to keep those howling devils beyond range of the main column, absorb their attention, pick up our wounded as we go, and be ready to give the warriors a welcome when they charge.

Kellogg, with Company "I," has driven back the attempted turn of our right, but the Indians keep up their harassing attack from the rear. Time is precious, and Upham begins to think we are wasting it. Again the Adjutant has come to him from General Carr, and now is riding along the line to the right, communicating some order to the officers, while Lieutenant Bishop is doing the same on the left. Just as the skirmishers cross the next ridge a few cool old shots from each company drop on hands and knees, and, crawling back to the crest, open a rapid fire on the pursuers, checking them. Covered by this the main line sweeps down at a run, crosses the low, boggy ground between them, and toils up the ridge on which we are stationed. Here they halt, face about, throw themselves flat on their faces, and the Major signals to the outlying skirmishers to come in; they obey with a rush, and a minute after a mass of Indians pops over the divide in pursuit. With a ringing hurrah of exultation our line lets drive a volley, the astonished redskins wheel about, those who can, lugging with them the dead or wounded who have fallen, and scatter off under shelter.

"How's that, King?" says the Major, with a grin. "Think they've had enough?" Apparently they have, as none reappear except in distant groups. Mount is the word. Ranks are formed, the men chat and laugh a moment, as girths and stirrups are being rearranged, then silence and attention as they break into column and jog off after Crook's distant battalions.

The Adjutant is jotting down the list of casualties in his notebook. "What time is it, Major?" "Eight o'clock," says Upham, wringing the wet from his hat. "Eight o'clock here; church time in Milwaukee."

Who would have thought it was Sunday?

TEN

BUFFALO BILL AND BUFFALO CHIPS

IN ALL THESE YEARS of campaigning, the Fifth Cavalry has had varied and interesting experiences with a class of men of whom much has been written, and whose names, to readers of the dime novel and *New York Weekly* style of literature, were familiar as household words; I mean the "Scouts of the Prairie," as they have been christened. Many a peace-loving citizen and thousands of our boys have been to see Buffalo Bill's thrilling representations on the stage of the scenes of his life of adventure. To such he needs no introduction, and throughout our cavalry he is better known than any general except Crook.

A motley set they are as a class—these scouts; hard-riding, hard-swearing, hard-drinking ordinarily, and not all were of unimpeachable veracity. But there was never a word of doubt or question in the Fifth when Buffalo Bill came up for discussion. He was chief scout of the regiment in Kansas and Nebraska in the campaign of 1868–69, when the hostiles were so completely used up by General Carr. He remained with us as chief scout until the regiment was ordered to Arizona to take its turn at the Apaches in 1871, and nothing but his having a wife and family prevented his going thither. Five years the regiment was kept among the rocks and deserts of that marvelous land of cactus and centipede;

but when we came homeward across the continent and were ordered up to Cheyenne to take a hand in the Sioux war of 1876, the first addition to our ranks was Buffalo Bill himself. He was "starring it" with his theatrical troupe in the far East, and read in the papers that the Fifth was ordered to the support of General Crook. It was Bill's benefit night at Wilmington, Delaware. He rushed through the performance, paid off his company, took the midnight express, and four days later sprang from the Union Pacific train at Cheyenne, and was speedily exchanging greetings with an eager group of his old comrades, reinstated as chief scout of the regiment.

Of his services during the campaign that followed, a dozen articles might be written. One of his best plays is founded on the incidents of our fight of the 17th of July with the Cheyenne Indians on the War Bonnet, for it was there he killed the warrior Yellow Hand in as plucky a single combat on both sides as is ever witnessed. The Fifth had a genuine affection for Bill; he was a tried and true comrade—one who for cool daring and judgment had no superior. He was a beautiful horseman, an unrivalled shot, and as a scout unequalled. We had tried them all—Hualpais and Tontos in Arizona; half-breeds on the great plains. We had followed Custer's old guide, "California Joe," in Dakota; met handsome Bill Hickox (Wild Bill) in the Black Hills; trailed for weeks after Crook's favorite, Frank Gruard, all over the Big Horn and Powder River country; hunted Nez Percés with Cosgrove and his Shoshones among the Yellowstone mountains, and listened to "Captain Jack" Crawford's yarns and rhymes in many a bivouac in the Northwest. They were all noted men in their way, but Bill Cody was the paragon.

105

This time it is not my purpose to write of him, but, *for* him, of another whom I've not yet named. The last time we met, Cody and I, he asked me to put in print a brief notice of a comrade who was very dear to him; and it shall be done now.

James White was his name, a man little known east of the Missouri; but on the Plains he was Buffalo Bill's shadow. I had met him for the first time at McPherson station in the Platte Valley, in 1871, when he came to me with a horse, and the simple introduction that he was a friend of Cody's. Long afterwards we found how true and stanch a friend, for when Cody joined us at Cheyenne as chief scout he brought White with him as assistant, and Bill's recommendation secured his immediate employment.

On many a long day's march after that White rode by my side along the flanks of the column, and I got to know him well. A simpler-minded, gentler frontiersman never lived. He was modesty and courtesy itself, conspicuous mainly because of two or three unusual traits for his class —he never drank, I never heard him swear, and no man ever heard him lie.

For years he had been Cody's faithful follower—half servant, half "pardner." He was Bill's *Fidus Achates;* Bill was his adoration. They had been boys together, and the hero worship of extreme youth was simply intensified in the man. He copied Bill's dress, his gait, his carriage, his speech—everything he could copy; he let his long yellow hair fall low upon his shoulders in wistful imitation of Bill's glossy brown curls. He took more care of Bill's guns and horses than he did of his own; and so, when he finally claimed one night at Laramie the right to be known by some other title than simple Jim White—something descrip-

106

tive, as it were, of his attachment for Cody and lifelong devotion to his idol "Buffalo Bill," a grim quartermaster (Morton, of the Ninth Infantry), dubbed him "Buffalo Chips," and the name was a fixture.

Poor, honest-hearted "Chips"! His story was a brief one after that episode. We launched out from Laramie on the 22d of June, and, through all the vicissitudes of the campaign that followed, he was always near the Fifth. On the Yellowstone Cody was compelled to bid us a reluctant farewell. He had theatrical engagements to meet in the fall, and about the end of August he started on General Terry's boat for Fort Buford and the States. "Chips" remained in his capacity as scout, though he seemed sorely to miss his "pardner."

It was just two weeks after that we struck the Sioux at Slim Buttes, something of which I told you in a former chapter. You may remember that the Fifth had ridden in haste to the relief of Major Mills, who had surprised the Indians away in our front early Saturday morning, had whipped them in panicky confusion out of their "tepees" into the neighboring rocks, and then had to fight on the defensive against ugly odds until we rode in to the rescue. As the head of our column jogged in among the lodges and General Carr directed us to keep on down to face the bluffs to the south, Mills pointed to a ravine opening out into the village, with the warning, "Look out for that gully; there are two or three wounded Indians hidden in there, and they've knocked over some of my men."

Everybody was too busy just then to pay much attention to two or three wounded Indians in a hole. We were sure of getting them when wanted. So, placing a couple of sentinels where they could warn stragglers away from its front, we formed line along the south and west of the captured village and got everything ready to resist the attack we knew they would soon make in full force.

General Crook had arrived on the scene, and, while we were waiting for "Lo" to resume the offensive, some few scouts and packers started in to have a little fun "rousting out them Injuns." Half a dozen soldiers got permission to go over and join in while the rest of us were hungrily hunting about for something to eat. The next thing, we heard a volley from the ravine, and saw the scouts and packers scattering for cover. One soldier held his ground—shot dead. Another moment, and it became apparent that not one or two, but a dozen Indians were crouching somewhere in that narrow gorge, and the move to get them out assumed proportions. Lieutenant Clark, of General Crook's staff, sprang into the entrance, carbine in hand, and a score of cavalrymen followed, while the scouts and others went cautiously along either bank, peering warily into the cave-like darkness at the head. A squad of newspaper correspondents, led by that reckless Hibernian, Finerty, of the *Chicago Times,* came tearing over, pencil in hand, all eagerness for items, just as a second volley came from the concealed foe, and three more of their assailants dropped, bleeding, in their tracks. Now our people were fairly aroused, and officers and men by dozens hurried to the scene. The misty air rang with shots, and the chances looked bad for those redskins. Just at this moment, as I was running over from the western side, I caught sight of "Chips" on the opposite crest. All alone, he was cautiously making his way, on hands and knees, towards the head of the ravine, where he could look down upon the Indians beneath. As yet he was protected from their fire by the bank itself—his lean form distinctly outlined against the eastern sky. He reached a stunted tree that grew on the very edge of the gorge, and there he halted, brought his rifle close under his shoulder in readiness to aim, and then raised himself slowly to his feet, lifted his head higher, higher, as he peered over. Suddenly a quick, eager light shone in his face, a sharp movement of his rifle, as though he were about to raise it to the shoulder, when, bang!—a puff of white smoke floated up from the head of the ravine, "Chips" sprang convulsively in the air, clasping his hands to his breast, and with one startled, agonizing cry, "Oh, my God, boys!" plunged heavily forward, on his face, down the slope—shot through the heart.

Two minutes more, what Indians were left alive were prisoners, and that costly experiment at an end. That evening, after the repulse of the grand attack of Roman Nose and Stabber's warriors, and, 'twas said, hundreds of Crazy Horse's band, we buried poor "Chips" with our other dead in a deep ravine. Wild Bill, California Joe, and Cosgrove have long since gone to their last account, but, among those who knew them, no scout was more universally mourned than Buffalo Bill's devoted friend, Jim White.

ELEVEN

THE "CHIEF" AND THE STAFF

WITH THE DEATH of our scout, Jim White, that eventful afternoon on the 9th of September, 1876, the skulking Indians in the ravine seemed to have fired their last shot. Several squaws were half-dragged, half-pushed up the banks, and through them the hidden foe were at last convinced that their lives would be spared if they would come out and surrender. Pending the negotiations, General Crook himself, with two or three staff officers, came upon the scene, and orders were given that the prisoners should be brought to him.

The time was, in the martial history of our country, when brigadier generals were as plentiful as treasury clerks—when our streets were ablaze with brilliant buttons, double rows and grouped in twos; when silver stars shone on many a shoulder, and every such luminary was the centre of half a score of brilliant satellites, the blue-and-gold aides-de-camp, adjutant-generals, etc., etc. But those were the dashing days of the late civil war, when the traditions of 1812 and Mexico were still fresh in the military mind, and when we were half-disposed to consider it quite the thing for a general to bedeck himself in all the splendor to be borrowed from plumes, epaulettes, and sashes, and, followed by a curveting train of attendants, to gallop forth and salute his opponent before opening the battle. They did it in 1812, and "Old Fuss and Feathers," as many in the army called Winfield Scott, would have pursued the same system in '47, but for the fact that bluff Zachary Taylor—"Old Rough and Ready"—had taken the initiative, and left all full-dress outfits east of the Río Grande.

We do things in a still more practical style nowadays, and, when it comes to fighting Indians, all that is ornamental in warfare has been left to them. An Indian of the Sioux or Cheyenne tribe, when he goes into battle, is as gorgeous a creature as vermilion, pigment, plumed war bonnet, glittering necklace, armlets, bracelets, and painted shield can make him. But here is a chance to see a full-fledged brigadier general of the United States Army and his brilliant staff in action—date, September 9th, 1876; place, a muddy ravine in far-western Dakota; campaign, the great Sioux war of that year. Now, fellow citizens, which is brigadier and which is private soldier in this crowd? It has gathered in not unkindly curiosity around three squaws who have just been brought into the presence of the "big white chief." You are taxpayers—you contribute to the support of the brigadier and the private alike. Presumably, therefore, having paid your money, you take your pick. I see you will need assistance. Very well, then. This utterly unpretending party—this undeniably shabby-looking man in a private soldier's light-blue overcoat, standing ankle-deep in mud in a far-gone pair of private soldier's boots, crowned with a most shocking bad hat, is Brigadier General George Crook of the United States Army. He commanded the Eighth Corps at Cedar Creek, and ever since the war closed has been hustled about the great West, doing more hard service and making less fuss about it than you suppose possible in the case of a brigadier general. He has spent the best days of his life, before and since the war, in the exile of the frontier. He has fought all the tribes on the western slope of the Rockies, and nearly all on the eastern side. Pitt River Indians sent an arrow through him in 1857, and since the day he took command against the Apaches in Arizona no white man's scalp would bring the price his would, even in the most impoverished tribe on the continent.

The rain is dripping from the ragged edge of his old white felt hat and down over his untrimmed beard as he holds out his hand to greet, Indian fashion, the first squaw whom the interpreter, Frank Gruard, is leading forward. Poor, haggard, terrified old wretch, she recognizes the big chief at once, and, springing forward, grasps his hand in both of hers, while her eyes mutely implore protection. Never having seen in all her life any reception but torture for prisoners, she cannot be made to believe, for some minutes, that the white man does not war that way. The other squaws come crowding after her, each eager to grasp the General's hand, and then to insert therein the tiny fist of the papoose hanging in stolid wonderment on her back. One of the squaws, a young and really handsome woman, is shot through the hand, but she holds it unconcernedly before her, letting the blood drip to the ground while she listens to the interpreter's explanation of the General's assurance of safety.

Standing by the General are two of his aides. West of the Missouri you would not need introduction to him or them, for no men are better known; but it is the rarest thing imaginable to see any one of the three anywhere else. In point of style and attire, they are no better off than their chief. Bourke, the senior aide and adjutant general of the expedition, is picturesquely gotten up in an old shooting coat, an indescribable pair of trousers, and a straw hat minus ribbon or binding, a brim ragged as the edge of a saw, and

112

a crown without a thatch. It was midsummer, you recollect, when we started on this raid, and, while the seasons have changed, our garments, perforce, remain the same, what there is left of them.

Schuyler, the junior, is a trifle more "swell" in point of dress. His hat has not quite so many holes; his hunting shirt of brown canvas has stood the wear and tear of the campaign somewhat better, and the lower man is garbed in a material unsightly but indestructible. All three are old campaigners in every part of the West. The third aide-de-camp we saw in the previous article, down in the ravine itself, heading the attack on the Indians. Clark is unquestionably the show figure of the staff, for his suit of Indian-tanned buckskin seems to defy the elements, and he looks as handsome and jaunty as the day we met him on the Yellowstone.

Meantime more Indians are being dragged out of their improvised rifle pits—warriors, squaws, and children. One of the latter is a bright-eyed little miss of some four or five summers. She is absolutely pretty, and looks so wet and cold and hungry that Bourke's big heart is touched, and, lifting her from the ground, he starts off with her towards where the Fifth Cavalry are bivouacked, and I go with them. The little maiden suspects treachery—torture or death, no doubt —for with all her savage strength, she kicks, struggles, claws and scratches at the kindly, bearded face, scorns all the soothing protestations of her captor, and finally, as we arrive at Bourke's campfire, actually tears off that veteran straw hat, and Bourke, being a bachelor, hands his prize over to me with the remark that, as a family man, I may have better luck. Apparently I do not, but in a moment the Adjutant General is busying himself at his haversack. He produces an almost forgotten luxury—a solid hardtack; spreads upon it a thick layer of wild-currant jam, and hands it to the little termagant who is deafening me with screams. "Take it, it's washtay, Wauwataycha"; and, sudden as sunburst from April cloud, little Wauwataycha's white teeth gleamed in smiles an instant, and then are buried in the sweet morsel. Her troubles are forgotten, she wriggles out of my arms, squats contentedly in the mud by the fire, finishes a square foot of hardtack in less time than we could masticate an inch, and smilingly looks up for more.

Poor little heathen! It wasn't the treatment she expected, and, doubtless, more than ever, she thinks "white man heap fool," but she is nonetheless happy. She will fill her own little stomach first, and then go and tell the glad tidings to her sisters, cousins, and aunts, and that white chief will have consequential damages to settle for scores of relatives of the original claimant of his hospitality. Indian logic in such matters is nothing if not peculiar. Lo argues, "You give my papoose something to eat—you my papoose friend; now you give me, or you my enemy."

Nothing but big luck will save Bourke's scanty supply of provender this muddy, rainy afternoon.

We have captured a dozen or more rabid Indians who but half an hour ago were strewing the hillside with our dead. Here's one grinning, hand-shaking vagabond with one of Custer's corporals uniforms on his back—doubtless that corporal's scalp is somewhere in the warrior's possession, but he has the deep sagacity not to boast of it; and no man in his sound senses wants to search the average Indian. They are our prisoners. Were we theirs, by this time we would be nakedly ornamenting a solid stake and broiling to a juicy death to the accompaniment of their exultant howls. But fate ordains otherwise; we are good North American citizens and must conciliate—so we pass them around with smiling, pacific grasp of hand— cheery "How coolahs," and seat them by the fire and bid them puff of our scanty store of tobacco and eat of our common stock of pony. But we leave a fair-sized guard with orders to perforate the first redskin that tries to budge, while the rest of us grab our carbines and hurry to our posts. Scattering shots are heard all along and around our line—the trumpets of the cavalry ring out "To Arms!" the Fifth Cavalry follows with "Forward." It means business, gentlemen, for here come Crazy Horse, Roman Nose, and scores, nay hundreds, of these Dick Turpins of the Plains, bent on recapturing their comrades. We must drop pen to meet them.

TWELVE

THE COMBAT OF SLIM BUTTES

IT IS A STIRRING SIGHT that meets the eye as, scrambling up from the shelter of the ravine in which we have been interviewing our captives, we gain the hillside and look hurriedly around. The whole landscape is alive with men and horses in excited motion. We are in a half-amphitheatre of picturesque and towering bluffs. North, south, and west they frown down upon us, their crests enveloped in eddying mist and rain clouds, the sward at their base rolling towards us in successive dips and ridges. Not three hundred yards away the nearest cliff tosses skyward directly south of the centre of the village we have won, but to the west and north they open out a good three-quarter-mile away.

The village itself consists of some thirty lodges or tepees of the largest and most ornate description known to Sioux architecture. The prisoners say that the head man of the municipality was Roman Nose, and that he and his band are but flankers of the great chieftain Crazy Horse, whose whereabouts are vaguely indicated as "over there," which may mean among the white crags of Slim Buttes, within rifleshot, or miles away towards the Little Missouri. The tepees are nestled about in three shallow ravines or "cooleys," as the Northern plainsmen sometimes call them, which, uniting in the centre of the metropolis, form a little valley through which their joint contributions trickle away in a muddy streamlet. On a point at the confluence of the two smaller branches stands a large lodge of painted skins, the residence no doubt of some chief or influential citizen, for it is chuck-full of robes and furs and plunder of every description. Here, not inside, for the domicile savors of long and unventilated occupation, but outside in the mud, General Carr has established the headquarters of the Fifth Cavalry. Its left is bivouacked directly in front, facing south in the narrow ravine nearest the tall white butte that stands like a sentinel against the stormy sky, while the rest of the line sweeps around to the west, crossing the level plateau between the two main ravines. Mason's battalion is holding this front and uniting with the Second Cavalry battalion on our right.

Directly behind us rises a mound in the very centre of our position, and here General Merritt, who commands the whole cavalry brigade, has planted his flag. It overlooks the field. Below him to the north are the lodges to which the wounded men have been brought and where the surgeons are now at work. Here, too, the compact battalion of the infantry has stacked its arms and set about kicking the heavy mud off its worn brogans. Somewhere over there also is the entire Third Cavalry, but I have been too busy with other entertainments since we trotted in at noon to find out much about them. To them belongs solely and entirely the honor of the capture of the village in the first place—only a hundred and fifty men at that. Their advance under Mills and Crawford, Schwatka and poor Von Luettwitz (who pays for the honor with a leg the surgeons have just lopped off) dashed in at daybreak while we were yet twenty miles away, and since we got in to help them hold the prize all hands have had their hands full.

Southeast of Merritt's central position a curling white smoke rising from the main ravine through the moisture-laden air, and begriming the folds of a red-and-blue head-quarters flag, indicates where Crook himself is to be found. The Brigadier is no better off—cares to be no better off than the private. He has not a rag of canvas to shelter his head.

Close in around the lines the lean, bony, leg-weary horses of the cavalry are herded, each company by itself where best it can find patches of the rich buffalo grass. No need to lariat those horses now. For weeks past they have barely been able to stagger along, and the morning's twenty-mile shuffle through the mud has utterly used them up. Nevertheless, each herd is strongly guarded; for the Indians are lurking all around us, eagerly watching every chance.

The scattering shots from the distant portion of our lines that have brought us scrambling up the hillside wake the scene to the instant life and excitement we note as we reach the first ridge. As adjutant, my duties call me at once to General Carr's headquarters, whence half a dozen officers who were gathered in conversation are scattering to their companies. A shout from the hillside announces, "Indians firing into the herds over in front of the Third Cavalry." Even as the hail is heard, a rattling of small arms, the sharp, vicious "ping" of the carbine and the deep "bang" of the longer-ranged rifle, sweeps along the western front. Just as we expected, Crazy Horse has come to the rescue, with all his available warriors. It is just half-past four o'clock by General Carr's watch, and between this and sunset the matter must be settled. As yet we can see nothing of it from our front, but every man seems to know what's coming. "Sound to Arms, Bradley," is General Carr's quiet order to our chief trumpeter, and as the ringing notes resound along the ravines the call is taken up from battalion to battalion. The men spring to ranks, the herd guards are hurrying in their startled horses, and the old chargers, scenting Indians and danger, toss their heads snorting in the air and come trotting in to their eager masters. All but one herd— "Look at the Grays," is the cry; for Montgomery's horses have burst into a gallop, excited by the shouts and clamor, and there they go up the slope, out to the front, and square into the fastness of the Indians. Not yet! A dozen eager troopers, officers and men, have flung themselves on their steeds, all without saddles, some without bridles, and are off in chase. No need of their services, though. That dragoon corporal in charge of the herd is a cool, practised hand— he *has* to be to wear chevrons in Montgomery's troop—and dashing to the front, he half leads, half turns the leaders over to the left, and in a great circling sweep of five hundred yards has guided them back into the very midst of their company. It is at once skilful and daring. No Indian could have done it better, and Corporal Clanton is applauded then and mentioned in General Carr's report thereafter.

Even as it is occurring, the hillsides in our own front bristle with the savage warriors, too far off as yet for close shooting, but threateningly near. Our horses must be kept under cover in the ravines, and the lines thrown out to meet the foe, so "Farward" is sounded. Upham's battalion scramble up the ridge in their front, and the fun begins. All around the rocky amphitheatre the Indians come bobbing into sight on their active ponies, darting from behind rocks and ledges, appearing for a brief instant over the rise of open ground eight hundred yards away, then as suddenly dipping out of sight into some intervening "swale," or depression. The first thing, while the General's horse and mine are being saddled, is to get the other animals into the ravine under shelter, and while I'm at it, Bourke, the aide-de-camp we last saw petting and feeding his baby-captive, comes rattling up the pebbly stream bed and rides out to the front with that marvellous wreck of a straw hat flapping about his ears. He never hears the laughing hail of "How did you leave your baby, John?" but is the first mounted officer I see along the line.

> *Press where you see my old hat shine,*
> *Amid the ranks of war,*
> *And be your oriflamme today*
> *This tile from Omaha.*

Macaulay barbarously paraphrased in the mud of Slim Buttes.

As the General swings into saddle and out to the front, the skirmish line is spreading out like a fan, the men running nimbly forward up the ridges. They are not well in hand, for they fire rapidly as they run. The volleys sound like a second Spottsylvania, a grand success as a *feu de joie,* but as the Colonel indignantly remarks, "They couldn't hit a flock of barns at that distance, much less an Indian skipping about like a flea," and orders are sent to stop the wild shooting. That there are hundreds of Indians is plainly apparent from their rapid fire, but they keep five or six hundred yards away behind the ridges, peppering at every exposed point of our line. Upham's battalion is swinging around to the west; Mason has pushed his five companies square out to the front along the plateau, driving the Indians before him. To his right the Second and Third Cavalry, fighting dismounted too, are making merry music. And now, filing over the ridge, comes the long column of infantry; and when they get to work with their "long toms" the Indians will have to skip in earnest. The shrill voice of their gray-bearded old chief sends his skirmishers rapidly out on Up-

ham's left, and a minute more the rocks are ringing with
the deeper notes of his musketry. Meantime I have counted
at least two hundred and fifty Indian warriors darting down
from one single opening among the bluffs square in Mason's
front, and the wounded are drifting in from his line far more
rapidly than from other exposed points. The brunt of the
attack coming along that plateau falls on him and his five
companies.

It is growing darker, and the flashes from our guns take
a ruddier tinge. The principal occupation of our officers,
staff and line, has been to move along among the men and
prevent the waste of ammunition. Every now and then some
young redskin, ambitious of distinction, will suddenly pop
from behind a sheltering hummock and dash at the top of
his pony's speed along our front, but over three hundred
yards away, taunting and blackguarding us in shrill vernacular as he does do. Then the whole brigade wants to let
drive at him and squander ammunition at the rate of five
dollars a second on that one pestiferous vagabond. "Hold
your fire, men!" is the order. "Give them half a chance and
some of the painted humbugs will ride in closer.

By 5:30 the light is so uncertain that we, who are facing
west along the plateau, and have the grim buttresses of the
Buttes in our front, can barely distinguish the scudding
forms of the Indians; but the flash of their rifles is incessant,
and now that they are forced back beyond the possibility of
harm to our centre, the orders are to lie down and stand
them off. These men crouching along the ridge are Company "F," of the Fifth. They and their captain (Payne)
you have heard more of in the Ute campaign. One of them,
a keen shot, has just succeeded in knocking an Indian out
of his saddle and capturing his pony, and even while his

comrades are shouting their congratulations, up comes Jack Finerty, who seeks his items on the skirmish line, and uses pencil and carbine with equal facility. Finerty wants the name of the man who killed that Indian, and, learning from the eager voices of the men that it is "Paddy" Nihil, he delightedly heads a new paragraph of his despatch "Nihil Fit," shakes hands with his brother Patlander, and scurries off to take a hand in the uproar on the left.

> *The war that for a space did fail*
> *Now trebly thundering swelled the gale.*

Colonel Chambers, with his plucky infantrymen, has clambered up the cliff on the south, changed front forward on his right—practically, not tactically—and got in a flank fire along the very depressions in which the Indians are settled. This is more than they can stand. The sun goes down at Slim Buttes on hundreds of baffled and discomfited Sioux. They have lost their village; lost three hundred tiptop ponies. A dozen of their warriors and squaws are in our hands, and a dozen more are dead and dying in the attempt to recapture them; and the big white chief Crook has managed to gain all this with starving men and skeleton horses.

Drawing in for the night, we post strong pickets well out in every direction, but they are undisturbed. Now comes the summing-up of casualties. The adjutants make the weary round of their regiments through wind and rain, taking the reports of company commanders, and then repairing to the surgeons to verify the lists. Two or three lodges have been converted into field hospitals; and in one of these, among our own wounded, two of the surgeons are turning their attention to a captive—the warrior American Horse. He lies upon some muddy robes, with the lifeblood ebbing from a ghastly hole in his side. Dr. Clements examines his savage patient tenderly, gently as he would a child; and, though he sees that nothing can save life, he does all that art can suggest. It is a painful task to both surgeon and subject. The latter scorns chloroform, and mutters some order to a squaw crouching at his feet. She glides silently from the tepee, and returns with a bit of hard stick; this he thrusts between his teeth, and then, as the surgeons work, and the sweat of agony breaks out upon his forehead, he bites deep into the wood, but never groans nor shrinks. Before the dawn his fierce spirit has taken its flight, and the squaws are crooning the death chant by his side.

Our own dead are fortunately few, and they are buried deep in the ravine before we move southward in the morning —not only buried deep, but a thousand horses, in column of twos, tramp over the new-made graves and obliterate the trace. You think this is but poor respect to show to a soldier's grave, no doubt; but then you don't know Indians, and cannot be expected to know that as soon as we are gone the skulking rascals will come prowling into the camp, hunting high and low for those graves; and, if they find them, will dig up the bodies we would honor, secure the scalps as trophies of their prowess, and then, after indescribable hackings and mutilations, consign the poor remains to their four-footed relatives, the prairie wolves.

Our wounded are many, and a hard time the patient fellows are having. Such rude shelter as their comrades can improvise from the Indian tepees we interpose between them and the dripping skies above. The raindrops sputter in the flickering watch fires around their cheerless bivouac; the night wind stirs the moaning pines upon the cliffs, and sweeps down in chill discordance through creaking lodgepoles and flapping roof of hide; the gaunt horses huddle close for warmth and shelter; the muffled challenge of the outlying picket is answered by the yelp of skulking coyote; and wet, cold, muddy, and, oh! so hungry, the victors hug their drenched blankets about their ears, and, grasping their carbines, pillowed on their saddles, sleep the sleep of the deserving.

THIRTEEN

A RACE FOR RATIONS

THE VILLAGE of Slim Buttes destroyed, General Crook pushed ahead on his southward march in search of the Black Hills and rations. All Sunday morning Upham's battalion of the Fifth Cavalry covered the rear and fought back the savage attacks upon the column; but, once well away from the smoking ruins, we were but little molested, and soon after noon caught up with the rest of the regiment and found the entire command going into bivouac along a little stream flowing northward from an opening among towering cliffs that were thrown like a barrier athwart our line of march. It was cold, cheerless, rainy weather, but here we found grass and water for our famished horses, plenty of timber for our fires, though we had not a thing to cook; but men and horses were weak and chilled and glad of a chance to rest.

Here Doctors Clements, Hartsuff, and Patzki, with their assistants, went busily to work perfecting the improvised transportation for the wounded. There was not an ambulance or a field litter in the command. Two officers—Bache of the Fifth and Von Luettwitz of the Third Cavalry—were utterly *hors de combat,* the latter having left his leg at the fight on the previous day, and some twenty-five men, more or less severely wounded, were unable either to walk or ride a horse.

Frontiersmen are quick to take lessons from the Indians, the most practical of transportation masters. Saplings twelve feet in length were cut (Indian lodgepoles were utilized); the slender ends of two of these were lashed securely on either side of a spare packmule, the heavy ends trailing along the ground, and fastened some three feet apart by crossbars. Canvas and blankets were stretched across the space between; hereon one wounded man was laid, and what the Indians and plainsmen call a *travois* was complete. Over prairie or rockless road it does very well, but for the severely wounded a far more comfortable litter was devised. Two mules were lashed "fore and aft" between two longer saplings; the intervening space was rudely but comfortably upholstered with robes and blankets, and therein the invalid might ride for hours as smoothly as in a palace car. Once, in the Arizona mountains, I was carried an entire week in a similar contrivance, and never enjoyed easier locomotion —so long as the mules behaved. But just here it may be remarked that comfort which is in the faintest degree dependent upon the uniform and steadfast serenity of the army mule is of most uncertain tenure. Poor McKinstry, our wagon master (who was killed in Payne's fight with the Utes last September, and whose unflattering comparison may have been provoked by unhappy experiences with the sex), used to say: "Most mules could swap ends quicker'n a woman could change her mind"; and it was by no means required that the mule should "swap ends" to render the situation of the poor fellow in the *travois* undesirable, if, indeed, he was permitted to retain it.

Sunday afternoon was spent in doing the little that could be done towards making the wounded comfortable, and the manufacture of rude leggins, moccasins, etc., from the skins captured from the Indians on the previous day. Sharp

A Sick Soldier on a "Travois"

lookouts were kept, but no enemy appeared. Evidently the Sioux were more than satisfied that Crook was worse than a badger in a barrel—a bad one to tackle.

Early on the morning of the 11th we climbed stiffly into saddle, and pushed on after our chief. Our way for some two miles or more led upgrade through wooded bluffs and heights. A dense fog hung low upon the landscape, and we could only follow blindly in the trail of our leaders. It was part of my duty to record each day's progress, and to sketch in my notebook the topography of the line of march. A compass was always in the cuff of my gauntlet, and notebook in the breast of my hunting shirt; but for three or four days only the trail itself, with streams we crossed and the heights within a mile or two of the flank, had been jotted down. Nothing further could be seen. It rained eleven days and nights without perceptible stop, and the whole country was flooded—so far as the mist would let us judge.

But this wretched Monday morning, an hour out from bivouac, we came upon a view I never shall forget. Riding along in the Fifth Cavalry column—every man wrapped in his own thoughts, and wishing himself wrapped in something warmer, all too cold and wet and dispirited to talk— we were aroused by exclamations of surprise and wonder among the troopers ahead. A moment more and we arrived in amaze at a veritable jumping-off-place, a sheer precipice, and I reined out to the right to dismount and jot down the situation. We had been winding along up, up, for over an hour, following some old Indian trail that seemed to lead to the moon, and all of a sudden had come apparently to the end of the world. General Crook, his staff and escort, the dismounted men and the infantry battalion away ahead had turned sharp to the left, and could be faintly seen winding off into cloudland some three hundred feet below. Directly in our front, to the south, rolling, eddying masses of fog were the only visible features. We were standing on the brink of a vertical cliff, its base lost in clouds far beneath. Here and there a faint breeze tore rents through the misty veil, and we caught glimpses of a treeless, shrubless plain beneath. Soon there came sturdier puffs of air; the sun somewhere aloft was shining brightly. We could neither see nor feel it—had begun to lose faith in its existence—but the clouds yielded to its force, and, swayed by the rising wind, drew away upward. Divested of the glow of colored fires, the glare of calcium light, the shimmering, spangled radiance of the stage, the symphony of sweet orchestra, we were treated to a transformation scene the like of which I have never witnessed, and never want to see again.

The first curtain of fog uplifting revealed rolling away five hundred feet beneath a brown barren, that ghastly compound of spongy ashes, yielding sand, and soilless soulless earth, on which even greasewood cannot grow, and sagebrush sickens and dies—the *mauvaises terres* of the French missionaries and fur traders—the curt "bad lands" of the Plains vernacular, the meanest country under the sun. A second curtain, rising farther away to the slow music of muttered profanity from the audience, revealed only worse and more of it. The third curtain exposed the same rolling barren miles to the southward. The fourth reached away to the very horizon, and vouchsafed not a glimpse of the longed-for Hills, nor a sign of the needed succor. Hope died from hungry eyes, and strong men turned away with stifled groans.

One or two of us there were who knew that, long before we got sight of the Black Hills, we must pass the Sioux landmark of "Deer's Ears"—twin conical heights that could be seen for miles in every direction, and even they were beyond range of my fieldglasses. My poor horse, ugly, rawboned, starved, but faithful "Blatherskite," was it in wretched premonition of your fate, I wonder, that you added your equine groan to the human chorus? You and your partner, "Donnybrook," were ugly enough when I picked you out of the quartermaster's herd at Fort Hays the night we made our sudden start for the Sioux campaign. You had little to recommend you beyond the facility with which you could rattle your heels like shillalahs about the ribs of your companions—a trait which led to your Celtic titles—but you never thought so poorly of your rider as to suppose that, after you had worn yourselves down to skin and bone in carrying him those bleak two thousand miles, he would help eat you; but he did—and it seemed like cannibalism.

Well! The story of that day's march isn't worth the telling. We went afoot, dragging pounds of mud with every step, and towing our wretched steeds by the bridle rein, envying the gaunt infantry, who had naught but their rifles to carry and could march two miles to our one. But late that afternoon, with Deer's Ears close at hand at last, we sank down along the banks of Owl Creek, the Heecha Wakpa of the Sioux, built huge fires, scorched our ragged garments, gnawed at tough horse meat, and wondered whether we really ever had tasted such luxuries as ham and eggs or porterhouse steak. All night we lay there in the rain; and at dawn Upham's battalion, with such horses as were thought capable of carrying a rider, were sent off downstream to the southeast on the trail of some wandering Indians who had crossed our front. The rest of us rolled our blankets and trudged out southward. It was Tuesday, the 12th of September, 1876—a day long to be remembered in the annals of the officers and men of the Big Horn and Yellowstone Expedition; a day that can never be thoroughly described, even could it bear description; a day when scores of our horses dropped exhausted on the trail—when starving men toiled piteously along through thick clinging mud or flung themselves, weeping and worn out, upon the broad, flooded prairie. Happily, we got out of the Bad Lands before noon; but one and all were weak with hunger, and as we dragged through boggy stream bed, men would sink hopelessly in the mire and never try to rise of themselves; *travois* mules would plunge frantically in bog and quicksand, and pitch the wounded screaming from their litters. I hate to recall it. Duties kept me with the rear guard, picking up and driving in stragglers. It was seven A.M. when we marched from Owl Creek. It was after midnight when Kellogg's rearmost files reached the bivouac along the Crow. The night was pitchy dark, the rain was pitiless; half our horses were gone, many of the men were scattered over the cheerless prairie far behind. But relief was at hand; the Belle Fourche was only a few miles away; beyond it lay the Black Hills and the stores of Crook City and Deadwood. Commissary and couriers had been sent ahead to hurry back provisions; by noon of the coming sun there would be abundance.

The morning came slowly enough. All night it had rained in torrents; no gleam of sunlight came to gladden our eyes or thaw the stiffened limbs of our soldiers. Crow Creek was running like a millrace. A third of the command had managed to cross it the evening before, but the rest had halted upon the northern bank. Roll call showed that many men had still failed to catch up; and an examination of the ford revealed the fact that, with precipitous banks above and below and deep water rushing over quicksands and treacherous bottom at the one available point, it must be patched up in some manner before a crossing could be effected. An orderly summoned me to the General's headquarters, and there I found him as deep in the mud as the rest of us. He simply wanted me to go down and put that ford into shape. "You will find Lieutenant Young there," said he, "and fifty men will report to you for duty." Lieutenant Young was there sure enough, and some fifty men did report, but there were no tools and the men were jaded; not more than ten or twelve could do a stroke of work. We hewed down willows and saplings with our hunting knives, brought huge bundles of these to the ford, waded in to the waist, and anchored them as best we could to the yielding bottom; worked like beavers until noon, and at last reported it practicable despite its looks. General Crook and his staff mounted and rode to the brink, but appearances were against us, and he plunged in to find a crossing for himself. Vigorous spurring carried him through, though twice we thought him down. But his horse scrambled up the opposite bank, the staff followed, dripping, and the next horseman of the escort went under, horse and all, and came sputtering to the surface at our shaky causeway, reached it in safety and floundered ashore. Then all stuck to our ford—the long column of cavalry, the wounded on their *travois* and the stragglers—and by two P.M. all were safely over. The Belle Fourche was only five miles away, but it took two good hours to reach it. The stream was broad, rapid, turbid, but the bottom solid as rock. Men clung to horses' tails or the stirrups of their mounted comrades, and were towed through; and then saddles were whipped off in a dense grove of timber, fires glowed in every direction, herd guards drove the weary horses to rich pastures among the slopes and hillsides south of the creek bottom, and all unoccupied men swarmed out upon the nearest ridge to watch for the coming wagons. Such a shout as went up when the cry was heard, "Rations coming." Such a mob as gathered when the foremost wagon drove in among the famished men. Guards were quickly stationed, but before that could be done the boxes were fairly snatched from their owner and their contents scattered through the surging crowd. Discipline for a moment was forgotten, men fought like tigers for crackers and plugs of tobacco. Officers ran to the scene and soon restored order, but I know that three gingersnaps I picked up from the mud under the horses' feet and shared with Colonel Mason and Captain Woodson—the first bite of bread we had tasted in three days—were the sweetest morsels we had tasted in years.

By five P.M. wagon after wagon had driven in. Deadwood and Crook City had rallied to the occasion. All they heard was that Crook's army had reached the Belle Fourche, starving. Our commissary, Captain Bubb, had bought at owners' prices all the bacon, flour, and coffee to be had. Local dealers had loaded up with every eatable item in their establishments. Company commanders secured everything the men could need. Then prominent citizens came driving out with welcoming hands and appreciated luxuries, and just as the sun went down Colonel Mason and I were emptying tin cups of steaming coffee and for two mortal hours eating flapjacks as fast as the cook could turn them out. Then came the blessed pipe of peace, warm, dry blankets, and the soundest sleep that ever tired soldier enjoyed. Our troubles were forgotten.

FOURTEEN

THE BLACK HILLS

IT WAS ON WEDNESDAY EVENING that our good friends, the pioneers of Deadwood and Crook City, reached us with their wagons, plethoric with all manner of provender; and the next day, as though in congratulation, the bright sunshine streamed in upon us, and so did rations. The only hard-worked men were the cooks, and from dawn to late at evening not an hour's respite did they enjoy. Towards sundown we caught sight of Upham's battalion coming in from its weary scout downstream. They had not seen an Indian, yet one poor fellow, Milner of Company "A," riding half a mile ahead of them in eager pursuit of an antelope, was found ten minutes after, stripped, scalped, and frightfully gashed and mutilated with knives, stone dead, of course, though still warm. Pony tracks were fresh in the springy sod all around him, but ponies and riders had vanished. Pursuit was impossible. Upham had not a horse that could more than stagger a few yards at a time. The maddest man about it was our Sergeant Major, Humme, an admirable shot and a man of superhuman nerve and courage; yet only a few months ago you read how he, with Lieutenant Weir, met a similar fate at the hands of the Utes. He fought a half-score of them singlehanded, and sent one of them to his final account before he himself succumbed to the missiles they poured upon him from their shelter in the rocks. A better soldier never lived, and there was grim humor in the statement of the eleven surviving Ute warriors, that they didn't want to fight Weir and Humme, but were obliged to kill them in self-defence. Weir was shot dead before he really saw the adversary, and those twelve unfortunate warriors, armed with their repeaters, would undoubtedly have suffered severely at the hands of Humme and his single shooter if they hadn't killed him too.

This is digressing, but it is so exquisitely characteristic of the Indian Bureau's way of doing things that, now that the peace commissioners have triumphantly announced that the attack on Thornburg's command was all an accident and have allowed the Indians to bully, temporize, and hoodwink them into weeks of fruitless delay (the rascals never meant to surrender the Meeker murderers so long as they had only peace commissioners to deal with), and now that, after all, the army has probably got to do over again what it started to do last October, and could readily have accomplished long ere this had they not been hauled off by the Bureau, the question naturally suggests itself, how often is this sort of thing to be repeated? Year after year it has been done. A small force of soldiers sent to punish a large band of Indian murderers or marauders. The small band has been well-nigh annihilated in many instances. Then the country wakes up, a large force concentrates at vast expense, and the day of retribution has come, when, sure as shooting, the Bureau has stepped in with restraining hand. No end of silk-hatted functionaries have hurried out from Washington, shaken hands and smoked a pipe with a score of big Indians; there has been a vast amount of cheap oratory and buncombe talk about the Great Father and guileless red men, at the end of which we are told to go back to camp and bury our dead, and our late antagonists, laughing in their sleeves, link arms with their aldermanic friends, are "dead-headed" off to Washington, where they are lionized at the White house and sent the rounds of the great cities, and finally return to their reservations laden down with new and improved rifles and ammunition, stovepipe hats, and Saratoga trunks, more than ever convinced that the one way to get what they want out of Uncle Sam is to slap his face every spring and shake hands in the fall. The apparent theory of the Bureau is that the soldier is made to be killed, the Indian to be coddled.

However, deeply as my comrades and myself may feel on this subject, it does not properly enter into a narrative article. Let us get back to Upham's battalion, who reached us late on the afternoon of the fourteenth, desperately tired and hungry. We lost no time in ministering to their wants, though we still had no grain for our horses, but the men made merry over abundant coffee, bacon and beans, and bread and molasses, and were unspeakably happy.

That evening the General decided to send back to the crossings of the swollen streams that had impeded our march on the 12th, and in which many horses and mules and boxes of rifle ammunition had been lost. Indians prowling along our trail would come upon that ammunition as the stream subsided, and reap a rich harvest.

The detail fell upon the Fifth Cavalry. One officer and thirty men to take the back track, dig up the boxes thirty miles away, and bring them in. With every prospect of meeting hundreds of the Sioux following our trail for abandoned horses, the duty promised to be trying and perilous, and when the Colonel received the orders from headquarters, and, turning to me, said, "Detail a lieutenant," I looked at the roster with no little interest. Of ten companies of the Fifth Cavalry present, each was commanded by its captain, but subalterns were scarce, and with us such duties were assigned in turn, and the officer "longest in" from scout or detachment service was Lieutenant Keyes. So that young gentleman, being hunted up and notified of his selection, girded up his loins and was about ready to start alone on his perilous trip, when there came swinging up to me an officer of infantry—an old West Point comrade who had obtained permission to make the campaign with the Fifth Cavalry and had been assigned to Company "I" for duty, but who was not detailable, strictly speaking, for such service as Keyes's from our roster. "Look here, King, you haven't given me half a chance this last month, and if I'm not to have this detail, I want to go with Keyes, as subordinate or anything; I don't care, only I want to go." The result was that he did go, and when a few days since we read in the *Sentinel* that Satterlee Plummer, a native of Wisconsin and a graduate of West Point, had been reinstated in the army on the special recommendation of General Crook, for gallantry in Indian campaign, I remembered this instance of the Sioux war of 1876, and, looking back to my notebook, there I found the record and result of their experience on the back track—they brought in fourteen horses and all the ammunition without losing a man.

Now our whole attention was given to the recuperation of our horses—the cavalryman's first thought. Each day we moved camp a few miles up the lovely Whitewood Valley, seeking fresh grass for the animals; and on September 18th we marched through the little hamlet of Crook City and bivouacked again in a beautiful amphitheatre of the hills, called Centennial Park. From here dozens of the officers and men wandered off to visit the mining gulches and settlements in the neighborhood, and numbers were taken prisoners by the denizens of Deadwood and royally entertained. General Crook and his staff, with a small escort, had left us early on the morning of the 16th to push ahead to Fort Laramie and set about the organization of a force for immediate resumption of business. This threw General Merritt in command of the expedition and meant that our horses should become the objects of the utmost thought and care. Leaving Centennial Park on the 19th, we marched southward through the Hills and that afternoon came upon a pretty stream named, as many another is throughout the Northwest, the Box Elder; and there we met a train of wagons guarded by spruce artillerymen fresh from their casemates on the seaboard, who looked upon our rags with undisguised astonishment, not unmixed with suspicion. But they were eagerly greeted, and that night, for the first time in four long weeks, small measures of oats and corn were dealt out to our emaciated animals. It was touching to see how carefully and tenderly the rough-looking men spread the precious morsels before their steeds, petting them the while and talking as fond nonsense to their faithful friends as ever mother crooned to sleeping child. It was only a bite for the poor creatures, and their eyes begged wistfully for more. We gave them two nights' rest, and then, having consumed all the grass to be had, pushed on to Rapid Creek, thence again to the southern limits of the Hills, passing through many a mining camp or little town with a name suggestive of the wealth and population of London. We found Custer City a deserted village—many a store and dozens of houses utterly untenanted. No forage to be had for love or money. Our horses could go no farther, so for weeks we lay along French Creek, moving camp every day or two a mile or more for fresh grass. It was dull work, but the men enjoyed it; they were revelling in plenty to eat and no drills, and every evening would gather in crowds around the campfires, listening

Deadwood City, Black Hills of Dakota

to some favorite vocalist or yarn spinner. Once in a while letters began to reach us from anxious ones at home and make us long to see them; and yet no orders came, no definite prospects of relief from our exile. At last, the second week in October started us out on a welcome raid down the valley of the South Cheyenne, but not an Indian was caught napping, and finally, on the 23d of October, we were all concentrated in the vicinity of the Red Cloud Agency to take part in the closing scene of the campaign and assist in the disarming and unhorsing of all the reservation Indians.

General MacKenzie with the Fourth Cavalry and a strong force of artillery and infantry was already there, and as we marched southward to surround the Indian camps and villages from the direction of Hat Creek our array was not unimposing, numerically. The infantry, with the "weak-horsed" cavalry, moved along the prairie road. Colonel Royall's command (Third Cavalry and Noyes's Battalion of the Second) was away over to the eastward, and well advanced, so as to envelope the doomed villages from that direction. We of the Fifth spread out over the rolling plain to the west, and in this order all moved towards Red Cloud, twenty odd miles away. It was prettily planned, but scores of wary, savage eyes had watched all Crook's preparations at the agency. The wily Indian was quick to divine that his arms and ponies were threatened, and by noon we had the dismal news by courier that they had stampeded in vast numbers. We enjoyed the further satisfaction of sighting with our glasses the distant clouds of dust kicked up by their scurrying ponies. A few rundred warriors, old men and "blanket Indians," surrendered to MacKenzie, but we of the Big Horn were empty-handed when once more we met our brigadier upon the following day.

140

FIFTEEN

DROPPED STITCHES

Now THAT an unlooked for interest had been developed in this enterprise of the Sunday *Sentinel,* and that in accordance with the wishes of many old comrades these sketches are reproduced in a little volume by themselves, many and many an incident is recalled which deserves to be noted but which was omitted for fear of wearying the readers for whom alone these stories of campaign life were originally intended; so that in this closing and retrospective chapter there will be nothing of lively interest, except to those already interested, and it can be dropped right here.

Looking back over it all, more especially the toilsome march and drenching bivouacs that followed the departure from Heart River, I wonder how some men stood it as they did. Among our own officers in the Fifth, one of our best and cheeriest comrades was Lieutenant Bache, "a fellow of infinite jest," and one to whom many of us were greatly attached. He was a martyr to acute rheumatism when he overtook us with Captains Price and Payne at the headquarters of the Mini Pusa. By the time we met General Terry on the Rosebud, he was in such agonizing helplessness as to be unable to ride a horse and was ordered to the Yellowstone and thence to Chicago for medical treatment; but while we lay at the mouth of the Powder River he suddenly reappeared in our midst, and, greatly benefited by the two weeks of rest and dry clothes on the boat, he insisted that he was well enough to resume duty. The surgeons shook their heads, but Bache carried his point with General Crook, and was ordered to rejoin the regiment. Then came day after day of pitiless, pouring rain, night after night unsheltered on the sodden ground. A cast-iron constitution would have suffered; poor Bache broke down, and, unable to move hand or foot, was lifted into a *travois* and dragged along. When we reached the Black Hills he was reduced to mere skin and bone, hardly a vestige of him left beyond the inexhaustible fund of grit and humor with which he was gifted. He reached Fort Dodge at the close of the campaign, but it had been too much for him. The news of his death was telegraphed by Captain Payne before we had fairly unsaddled for the winter.

Though brother officers in the same regiment, so are our companies scattered at times that before this campaign Bache and I had met but once, and that was in Arizona. Today the most vivid picture I have in my mind of that trying march in which he figures is a duck-hunting scene that I venture to say has never been equalled in the experience of Eastern sportsmen. We had halted on the evening of September 7th on the dripping banks of one of the forks of the Grand River (Palanata Wakpa, the Sioux call it, and a much better name it is), a muddy stream, not half the width of our Menominee, but encased between precipitous banks, and swirling in deep, dark pools. The grass was abundant, but not a stick of timber could we find with which to build a fire. While I was hunting for a few crumbs of hardtack in my lean haversack, there came a sudden sputter of pistol shots on the banks of the stream, and I saw scores of men running, revolver in hand, to the scene. Joining them, I found Bache reclining in his *travois* and blazing away at some objects in the pool below him. The surface of the Grand River (Palanata Wakpa, the Sioux call it, and a regiment of ravenous men was opening fire upon them with calibre-45 bullets. Only fancy it! The wary, gamy bird we steal upon with such caution in our marshes at home, here on the distant prairies, far from the busy haunts of men, so utterly untutored by previous danger, or so utterly bewildered by the fusillade, that hardly one took refuge in flight, while dozens of them, paddling, ducking, diving about the stream, fell victims to the heavy revolver, and, sprinkled with gunpowder for salt, were devoured almost raw by the eager soldiery. "Great Caesar's ghost," said Bache, as he crammed fresh cartridges into the chambers of his Colt, "what would they say to this on the Chesapeake?"

Another scene with Bache was at Slim Buttes. In order to prevent indiscriminate pillage among the captured lodges of the Sioux, General Crook had ordered the detail of guards to keep out the crowd of curiosity seekers. Bache was lying very stiff and sore near one of the large tepees, and I had stopped to have a moment's chat with him when something came crawling out of a hole slashed in the side by the occupants to facilitate their escape when Lieutenant Schwatka charged the village that morning; something so unmistakably Indian that in a second I had brought my revolver from its holster and to full cock. But the figure straightened up in the dim twilight, and with calm deliberation these words fell from its lips: "There ain't a thing worth having in the whole d——d outfit."

Bache burst into amused laughter. "Well, my aboriginal friend, who in thunder are you, anyhow? Your English is a credit to civilization."

It was "Ute John," one of the scouts who had joined us with the Shoshones on the Big Horn, but who, unlike them, had concluded to stand by us through the entire expedition. He was a tall, stalwart fellow, picturesquely attired in an overcoat not unlike our present unsightly ulster in shape, but made of a blanket which had been woven in imitation of numerous rainbows. The storied coat of many colors worn by the original Joseph was never more brilliant than this uncouth garment, and about this time an effort was made to rechristen our sturdy ally and call him no longer monosyllabic and commonplace John, but Scriptural Joseph. Subsequent developments in his career, however, brought about a revulsion of feeling, as it was found that the fancied resemblance in characteristics ended with the coat.

We had been accustomed in our dealings with the Indians who accompanied us to resort to pantomime as a means of conversation. Some of our number prided themselves on their mute fluency—none more so, perhaps, than our genial friend Major Andy Burt of the 9th Infantry, who would "buttonhole," so to speak, any Indian who happened along during his unoccupied moments, and the two would soon be lost in a series of gyrations and finger flippings that was a dark mystery to the rest of the command; and when the Major would turn triumphantly towards us with his "He says it's all serene, fellows," we accepted the information as gospel truth without asking what "it" was. Bache and I were not a little astonished, therefore, at hearing Ute John launch forth into fluent English, albeit strongly tinged with Plains vernacular.

The most tireless men in pursuit of Indian knowledge were the correspondents of the papers. Frequent mention has already been made of Mr. Finerty of the *Chicago Times,* who was the gem of the lot; but the *New York Times* and *Herald* were represented, as were leading journals of other

144

large cities. They proved excellent campaigners, and welcome, indeed genial, associates. The contrary impression
concerning one of them, to which expression was given in a
previous edition of this work, was due to a misunderstanding
since corrected. The exception made was that of the representative of a great metropolitan daily whose sharp criti-
cisms of our chief, and whose report of the morning affair
at Slim Buttes, had so angered many old comrades of mine
that for a long time after the paper reached us in our bivouac
among the Hills I heard nothing but denunciation of the
writer and most unflattering details of his conduct under
fire. Previous to that time my own knowledge of him was
derived from a laughing and by no means unkindly description given me by Dr. McGillicuddy; but after Slim Buttes,
and after his departure from among us, there were on every
side officers, troopers, and packers eager to tell what they
knew—and many, I have since found, what they did not
know—about this particular journalist. The officers who
were with Colonel Mills in the morning fight signed a protest
against the account which he had written, and both the
Herald and "Mr. D——" subsequently made entire retraction; but the impressions of the correspondent left on
my mind by the closing events of the campaign were of a
most unfavorable character. And so, when these sketches
were written three years afterwards, I told of "Mr. D——"
just as he had been described to me by many a comrade
who professed to know whereof he spoke.

I have since had reason to regret this far more deeply
than I can express. For ten years the statement went un-
challenged. It was only last October that the gentleman himself came upon the book and promptly demanded its withdrawal from sale, as it contained a libel that pointed directly
to him. The investigation made by his efforts and by mine

brought to light some curious facts which need not be detailed here, but I found enough to convince me that in accusing him of cowardice, my numerous authorities had very flimsy ground to stand on. Captain Charles Morton, of the Third Cavalry, assured me that this very correspondent rode by his side on the fighting line at the Rosebud (June 17th) and bore himself with cool courage. Colonel Dodge, who commanded the expedition of '75, wrote me that he had to rebuke him for recklessness; and Colonel Anson Mills himself, who had most reason to feel aggrieved at this correspondent, wrote me finally that he thought the accusation of cowardice should be withdrawn. As complete a retraction and apology as lay in my power to write was thereupon placed in the hands of Colonel W. C. Church, of the *Army and Navy Journal,* and it was accepted in a letter as courteous as could possibly be asked.

This practically closed the controversy, but I feel that it is due the gentleman referred to that these pages should contain a refutation of that charge of cowardice as positive as the original statement. We heard long after the campaign that he had been very ill at Cheyenne, but I, at least, did not know how ill and exhausted he was that wretched, dripping night before Mills's attack on the Indian village. There can be no further doubt that any reflection on the courage of "Mr. D——" or on his conduct as a gentleman was absolutely unjustifiable.

Once fairly in the Black Hills, and resting on the banks of French Creek, we set to work to count up the losses of the campaign. In horseflesh and equipments the gaps were appalling. Some companies in the Fifth were very much reduced, and, of course, when the horse dropped exhausted on the trail, there was no transportation for the saddle, bridle, and "kit." It often happened that for days the soldier led his horse along the flanks of the column or in the rear of the regiment, striving hard to nurse his failing strength, hunting eagerly for every little bunch of grass that might eke out his meagre subsistence. In all the array of company losses there was one, and only one, shining contrast— Montgomery, with Company "B," the Grays, calmly submitted a clear "bill of health"; he had not lost a single horse, which was marvellous in itself, but when "Monty" proceeded to state that every Company "B" man had his saddle, bridle, nose bag, lariat, picket pin, side lines, etc., the thing was incomprehensible; that is, it seemed incomprehensible until the fact was taken into consideration that those companies which bivouacked on either flank of the Grays woke each morning to the realization of a predatory ability on the part of "them d——d Company 'B' fellers" that rose superior to any defensive devices they might invent. But Company "B" could not acquire gray horses at the expense of the rest of the regiment, whatever it might have done in side and other lines, and the fact that Captain "Monty" paraded every horse with which he started is due to the unerring judgment and ceaseless vigilance with which he noted every symptom of weakness in any and every animal in his troop and cared for it accordingly.

As a rule, our company commanders are not thorough horsemen, and too little attention is devoted to the instruction of our cavalry officers in the subject—but Montgomery is a noteworthy exception. I don't know which class will be the more inclined to think me in error in the following statement, but as a result of not a little observation it is my opinion that, while the best riders in the cavalry service come from West Point, the best horsemen are from the ranks.

But for our anxiety about our horses, the most enjoyable

days of the campaign were probably contained in the first two weeks of October. We were the roughest-looking set of men on the face of the globe; but with abundant rations and rousing big fires along the valley of French Creek, with glad letters from home, and finally the arrival of our wagons with the forgotten luxuries of tents and buffalo robes, we began taking a new interest in life. The weather was superb, the sun brilliant, the air keen and bracing, the nights frostily cold. Wonderful appetites we had in those days, and after supper the men would gather in crowds around the camp-fires and sing their songs and smoke their pipes in placid contentment. The officers, too, had their reunions, though vocalists were scarce among them, and the proportions of "youngsters" who keep the fun alive was far too small. The year before, those irrepressible humorists, Harrigan and Hart, of the New York stage, had sung at their "Théâtre Comique" a witty but by no means flattering ditty which they called "The Regular Army, O." One of its verses, slightly modified to suit the hearers, was particularly applicable to and popular in the Fifth Cavalry, and their adjutant, when he could be made to sing *pro bono publico,* was always called upon for the song and sure of applause at the close of this verse. It ran:

> *We were sent to Arizona, for to fight the Indians there;*
> *We were almost snatched bald-headed, but they didn't*
>   *get our hair.*
> *We lay among the cañons and the dirty yellow mud,*
> *But we seldom saw an onion, or a turnip, or a spud,*
> *Till we were taken prisoners and brought forninst*
>   *the chief;*
> *Says he, "We'll have an Irish stew"—the dirty Indian*
>   *thief.*

Dropped Stitches

On Price's telegraphic wire we slid to Mexico,
And we blessed the day we skipped away from the
  Regular Army, O.

Now General Crook received his promotion to brigadier generalship in Arizona after a stirring and victorious campaign with the Apaches, and the Fifth Cavalry used to boast at times that his "star" was won for him by them. Soldiers are quick to attach some expressive nickname to their officers, but I never learned that our General had won this questionable distinction until we joined him at Goose Creek, when we found that in the command already there he was known as "Rosebud George."

In the hard times that followed there was no little growling among the half-starving troopers, because the packers seemed to have sufficient to eat when we were well-nigh destitute. So one night a fifth verse was trolled out on the still evening air in a strongly Hibernian brogue, and the listening ears of the Fifth were greeted with something like this:

But 'twas out upon the Yellowstone we had the
  d——dest time,
Faix, we made the trip wid Rosebud George, six
  months without a dime.
Some eighteen hundred miles we went through hunger,
  mud, and rain,
Wid backs all bare, and rations rare, no chance for
  grass or grain;
Wid 'bunkies shtarvin' by our side, no rations was the
  rule;
Shure 'twas ate your boots and saddles, you brutes, but
  feed the packer and mule.

*But you know full well that in your fights no soldier
  lad was slow,*
*And it wasn't the packer that won ye a star in the
  Regular Army, O.*

With full stomachs, however, came forgetfulness of suffering, and this with other campaign lyrics was forgotten.

It seemed so good to rest in peace for day after day.
General Merritt with his staff, and Major Upham, had
pitched their tents in the shelter of a little rocky promontory
that jutted out into the valley and was crowned by a sparse
growth of pines and cedars. One evening, as the full moon
shone down upon the assembled party over this ridge, a
perfectly defined cross appeared upon the very face of the
luminary. Everyone noticed it, and one of the number,
clambering to the summit, found growing from a cleft in the
rock a sturdy little leafless branch about two feet in length,
crossed by another and smaller twig; the cross was perfect,
and the effect in the moonlight something simply exquisite.
"Camp Faith" was thereupon selected as the name of cavalry headquarters. Somebody wanted a name for the Fifth
Cavalry camp, and, in recognition of our present blissful
and undisturbed existence as compared with recent vicissitudes, and mindful of the martial palace of Sans Souci at
Potsdam, a wildly imprudent subaltern suggested *Sans Sioux
Ici,* but it was greeted with merited contempt.

Of course all were eager for intimation of our next move.
Occasional despatches reached General Merritt, but not
a hint could be extracted from him. Rumors of a winter
campaign were distressingly prevalent, and the Fifth were
beginning to look upon a prolonged stay in the Hills as a
certainty, when one day an aide-de-camp of the Chief's

"The Dandy Fifth"
General Merritt and His Officers on the Sioux Campaign

came to me with the request that I would make a map for him of the country between the South Cheyenne and Red Cloud Agency, and let no one know what I was doing. A week after he wanted another sketch of the same thing, and it became evident, to me at least, that before very long we would be down along the White River, looking after "Machpealota."

The campaign itself being virtually over, the recruits authorized by special act of Congress to be enlisted for the cavalry regiments actively engaged began to be heard of at the front, and one evening in early October we learned that some four hundred heroes were on the march from Fort Laramie to join the Fifth, and that the Third was to be similarly reinforced. A hint as to the probable character of the new levies was also in circulation. Twenty-five hundred men having been suddenly and urgently needed, the recruiting officers were less particular in their selections than would otherwise have been the case, and from the purlieus of Philadelphia, Baltimore, and New York the scum of the country was eagerly grasping this method of getting to the Black Hills at Uncle Sam's expense. They were marching up to join us under the command of Captain Monahan of the Third Cavalry, assisted by Lieutenants Ward, Cherry, and Swift, "of Ours"; and on the 11th of October General Merritt struck camp, the "B., H., and Y.," horse, foot, and dragoon, bade farewell to French Creek, and, after an exhilarating ride through a wildly beautiful and picturesque tract of the Hills, we unsaddled, pitched our tents along Amphibious Creek, and that evening the new levies arrived. Nobody cared particularly to see the recruits, but the Fifth Cavalry turned out to a man to see the new horses; and having called upon and extended a welcoming hand to the comrades joining us for the first time, we made a dash for the quadrupeds. Before tattoo that evening there was not one that had not been closely inspected and squabbled over by the company commanders and their men, and the first thing the next morning General Merritt ordered the distribution of horses, "according to color," to companies.

It was revealed that an expedition somewhere was intended by his directing the regimental Adjutant to pick out the old soldiers among the recruits, assign them to companies at once, and then issue orders to the regiment to be in readiness to move at daybreak.

Never in my life have I seen such an array of vagabonds as that battalion of four hundred "unassigned" when I got them into line on the morning of the 12th of October and proceeded to "pick out the old soldiers" as directed. That was a matter of no difficulty; they were already acting as noncommissioned officers of the recruit companies, but were not sixty all told, and more were needed. Stopping before a sturdily built little fellow with a grizzled moustache and an unmistakably soldierly carriage, the only promising-looking man left in the three hundred who had "stood fast" when the order was given "men who have served previous enlistments step to front," the Adjutant questioned:

"Haven't you served before?"

"Not in the regulars, sir."

"That man is lame, sir," interposed a sergeant.

"It is an old wound," says the man eagerly, "and it's only so once in while. I can ride first-rate."

"What was your regiment?"

"Seventh Wisconsin, sir."

"What! Were you at Gainesville?"

"Yes, sir. Wounded there."

A knot of officers—Merritt, Mason, Sumner, and Montgomery—who fought through the war with the Army of the Potomac, are standing there as the Adjutant turns.

"Sergeant, take this man to Company "K" and fit him out—and—stop a moment. Bring him to my tent tonight after supper. Gentlemen, that's an Iron Brigade man."

That evening a Company "K" sergeant scratches the flap of the Adjutant's tent—you cannot knock when there is no door—and presents himself with the recruit-veteran. The latter looks puzzled but perfectly self-possessed; answers without hesitation two or three rapidly propounded questions as to names of his regimental officers in '62, and then seems completely bewildered as the Adjutant takes him cordially by the hand and bids him welcome. However, it did not require many words to explain the matter.

To return to those recruits. If the police force of our large Eastern cities were at a loss to account for the disappearance of a thousand or more of their "regular boarders," a flying trip to the Black Hills on this 12th day of October, '76, would have satisfied them as to their whereabouts. Where there were ten "good men and true" among the newcomers, there were forty who came simply with the intention of deserting when they got fairly into the Hills and within striking distance of the mines, an intention most successfully carried out by a large proportion of their number.

And then the names under which they enlisted! "What's your name?" said the Adjutant to the most unmistakable case of "Bowery Boy" in the front rank.

"My name's Jackson Bewregard," is the reply, with the accompaniment of hunching shoulders, projecting chin, overlapping underlip, and sneering nostril characteristic of Chatham Square in the palmy days of Mose.

"And yours?" to Mr. Bewregard's left file, a big rough of Hibernian extraction.

"My name's Jooles Vern."

The Adjutant glances at the muster roll: " 'No. 173— Jules Verne.' Ha! Yes. The party that wrote *Around the World in Eighty Days*. Have we many more of these eminent Frenchmen, sergeant?"

The sergeant grins under his great moustache. Possibly he is recalling a fact which the Adjutant has by no means forgotten; that ten years before, when they were both in General Billy Graham's famous light battery of the First Artillery, of which the Adjutant was then second lieutenant, the sergeant was then, too, a sergeant, but with a very different name.

Friday, October 13th—ill-omened day of the week, ill-omened day of the month—and we were to start on a scout down into the valley of the Cheyenne. Perhaps three fourths of our number neither knew nor cared what day it was; but, be that as it may, there was an utterly unmistakable air of gloom about our move. The morning was raw and dismal. "The General" sounded soon after nine, and the stirring notes fell upon seemingly listless ears; no one seemed disposed to shout, whistle, or sing, and just at ten o'clock, when we were all standing to horse and ready to start, Major Sumner's company sent forth a mournful little procession towards the new-made grave we had marked on the hillside at the sharp bend of the creek, and with brief service, but sad enough hearts, the body of a comrade who had died the night before was lowered to its rest. The carbines rang out the parting volleys, and Bradley's trumpet keened a wailing farewell. General Merritt and his staff, coming suddenly upon us during the rites, silently dismounted and uncovered until the clods rattled in upon the soldier's rude coffin, and all was over. Then, signalling us to follow, the Chief rode on; the Fifth swung into saddle, and with perceptibly augmented ranks followed in his tracks. A battalion of the Third Cavalry under Colonel Van Vliet and a detachment of the Second under Captain Peale accompanied us, while the infantry battalion, the rest of the cavalry, the recruits, and the sick or disabled remained in camp under command of Colonel Royall. Where were we going? What was expected? None knew behind the silent horseman at the head of column; but a start on Friday, the 13th, to the mournful music of a funeral march, boded ill for success. However, not to be harrowing, it is as well to state right here that ten days from that date the scout was over, and, without having lost man or horse, the Fifth rode serenely into Red Cloud Agency. So far as the regiment was concerned that superstition was exploded.

The march down Amphibious Creek was grandly beautiful as to scenery. We wound, snake-like, along the stream, gliding under towering, pine-covered heights, or bold, rocky precipices. The valley opened out wider as we neared the "sinks," and, finally, turning abruptly to the right, we dismounted and led our horses over a lofty ridge, bare of trees, and commanding a broad valley to the south, over which the road stretched in long perspective till lost in dark Buffalo Gap, the only exit through the precipitous and lofty range that hemmed in the plain between us and the Cheyenne Valley beyond. Here we encountered an emigrant train slowly toiling up the southern slope and staring at us in undisguised wonderment. Ten miles away we came once again "plump" upon the boiling waters of the creek, where it reappeared after a twelve-mile digression in the bowels of the

earth. It was clear and fair when it left us in the valley behind to take its plunge, and it met us again with a more than
troubled appearance and the worst kind of an odor. Square
in between the massive portals of the great gap we unsaddled at sunset and encamped for the night.

In the scout which ensued down the valley of the South
Cheyenne there was absolutely nothing of sufficient interest
to record in these pages. Nor had we any luck in our par-
ticipation in the "roundup" at the Indian reservation on the
22d and 23d of October. Such warriors as had remained
near Camp Robinson meekly surrendered to General Mac-
Kenzie, and we had nothing to do but pitch our tents side
by side with the newcomers of the Fourth Cavalry and
wonder what was to come next. General Crook was known
to be in the garrison with his aides-de-camp, and we had
not long to wait. On the 24th of October our motley array
received the welcome order to go into winter quarters, the
Fifth Cavalry on the line of the Union Pacific Railroad, and
within another twenty-four hours we were en route for the
comforts of civilization.

But, before we separated from the comrades with whom
we had marched and growled these many weary miles, our
Chief gave us his parting benediction in the following words:

> HEADQUARTERS BIG HORN AND
> YELLOWSTONE EXPEDITION,
> CAMP ROBINSON, NEB., OCTOBER 24, 1876

GENERAL ORDERS NO. 8

The time having arrived when the troops composing
the Big Horn and Yellowstone Expedition are about to
separate, the brigadier general commanding addresses
himself to the officers and men of the command to say:

In the campaign now closed he has been obliged to

call upon you for much hard service and many sacrifices of personal comfort. At times you have been out of reach of your base of supplies; in most inclement weather you have marched without food and slept without shelter; in your engagements you have evinced a high order of discipline and courage; in your marches, wonderful powers and endurance; and in your deprivations and hardships, patience and fortitude.

Indian warfare is, of all warfare, the most dangerous, the most trying, and the most thankless. Not recognized by the high authority of the United States Senate as war, it still possesses for you the disadvantages of civilized warfare, with all the horrible accompaniments that barbarians can invent and savages execute. In it you are required to serve without the incentive to promotion or recognition; in truth, without favor or hope of reward.

The people of our sparsely settled frontier, in whose defence this war is waged, have but little influence with the powerful communities in the East; their representatives have little voice in our national councils, while your savage foes are not only the wards of the nation, supported in idleness, but objects of sympathy with large numbers of people otherwise well-informed and discerning.

You may, therefore, congratulate yourselves that, in the performance of your military duty, you have been on the side of the weak against the strong, and that the few people there are on the frontier will remember your efforts with gratitude.

If, in the future, it should transpire that the avenues[1]

---

[1] The avenue was at last opened by the signature of the President to the bill providing that brevet rank might be conferred on officers for gallant conduct in Indian warfare, but it came just too late. General Crook had barely time to express his gratification. He died within the week that followed, and his list of officers recommended for brevets for services rendered in this campaign died with him.

for recognition of distinguished services and gallant conduct are opened, those rendered in this campaign will be remembered.

BY COMMAND OF BRIGADIER GENERAL CROOK
(Signed)

JOHN G. BOURKE,
FIRST LIEUTENANT THIRD CAVALRY,
A.D.C., AND A.A.A. GENERAL

To use the emphatic vernacular of the frontier, that parting order "just filled the bill." It was as complete a summing-up of the disadvantages of Indian campaigning as could well be written; it indicated plainly how thoroughly our General had appreciated the sufferings of his men on that hideous march from Heart River; it assured us of the sympathy he had felt for one and all (though I doubt if ever a one of us suffered half so much as he); and, finally, in tendering the thanks of our commander, it conveyed the only reward we could possibly expect, for had he not truly said that, of all warfare, Indian warfare is the most thankless?

Well, it was over with, so far as we were concerned, though brief was our respite, and now came the closing scenes before the rising of the morning's sun should see us split up into battalions or detachments, and, with light feet and lighter hearts, marching away to the south.

All night long, at General Crook's headquarters, his tireless staff were working away at orders and details of the move, and closing his report to the Lieutenant General at Chicago; and here, too, my services were kept in requisition preparing the map which was to accompany the written report, so that, for us at least, there was no opportunity of sharing in the parting festivities and bidding farewell to comrades, cavalry and infantry, separating for the new posts and the duties of recuperation.

Our farewells were hurried, yet even now, how vividly I recall the faces that crowded round headquarters that bright morning of the 25th. Bronzed and bearded, rugged with the glow of health, or pallid from wounds and illness, but all kindly and cordial. Then, too, the scenes of our campaign seemed passing in review before me, and, dreamlike, they linger with me still. Glancing over these now completed pages, how utterly meagre and unsatisfactory the record seems; how many an incident have I failed to mention; how many a deed of bravery or self-denial is left untold. I look back through the mists and rain into the dark depths of that bloody ravine at Slim Buttes, and wonder how I could ever have told the story of its assault and failed to speak of how our plucky Milwaukee sergeant sprang down in the very face of the desperately fighting Indians and picked up a wounded Third Cavalryman and carried him on his back out of further harm's way; and of brave, noble-hearted Munson, as true a soldier as ever commanded company, rushing in between two fires to drag the terrified squaws from their peril; of Bache, "swollen, puffed, and disfigured with rheumatism, conquering agony to mount his horse and take part in the action"; of Rodgers, striding down the slopes in front of his skirmish line, his glorious voice ringing above the clamor, laughing like a schoolboy at the well-meant efforts of the Indian sharpshooters to pick him off; of General Carr, riding out to the front on his conspicuous gray, and sitting calmly there to show the men what wretched shots some Indians could be.

How could half the incidents be told when so little parade was made of them at the time? Who knew the night of the stampede on the Rosebud that Eaton was shot through the hand until he had spent an hour or more completing his duties, riding as though nothing had happened? Who knew, at the Rosebud battle, that Nickerson's exertions in the saddle had reopened the old Gettysburg wound and well-nigh finished him? We thought he looked white and wan when he rejoined us at Red Cloud, but never divined the cause. From first to last throughout that march of eight hundred miles, so varied in its scenes, but so utterly changeless in discomfort, there was a spirit of uncomplaining "take-it-as-a-matter-of-course" determination that amounted at times among the men to positive heroism. Individual pluck was thoroughly tested, and the instances of failure were few and far between.

Despite the fact that our engagements were indecisive at the time (and Indian fights that fall short of annihilation on either side generally are), the campaign had its full result. Sitting Bull's thousands were scattered in confusion over the Northwest, he himself driven to a refuge "across the line," his subordinates broken up into dejected bands that, one after another, were beaten or starved into submission, and in the following year General Crook's broad department, the grand ranges of the Black Hills and Big Horn, the boundless prairies of Nebraska and Wyoming, were as clear of hostile warriors as, two years before, they were of settlers, and today the lovely valleys of the North, thanks to his efforts and the ceaseless vigilance of Generals Terry and Miles in guarding the line, are the peaceful homes of hundreds of hardy pioneers.

SERVING WITH THE FIFTH CAVALRY IN THE BIG HORN AND YELLOWSTONE EXPEDITION OF 1876

Colonel WESLEY MERRITT, Brevet Major General.

Lieutenant Colonel EUGENE A. CARR, Brevet Major General.

Major JOHN J. UPHAM.

Major JULIUS W. MASON, Brevet Lieutenant Colonel.

Captain EDWARD H. LEIB, Brevet Lieutenant Colonel.

Captain SAMUEL S. SUMNER, Brevet Major.

Captain EMIL ADAM.

Captain ROBERT H. MONTGOMERY.

Captain SANFORD C. KELLOGG, Brevet Lieutenant Colonel.

Captain GEORGE F. PRICE.

Captain EDWARD M. HAYES.

Captain J. SCOTT PAYNE.

Captain ALBERT E. WOODSON.

Captain CALBRAITH P. RODGERS.

First Lieutenant BERNARD REILLY, JR.

First Lieutenant WM. C. FORBUSH, A. A.G. Cavalry Brigade.

First Lieutenant CHARLES KING, Adjutant.

First Lieutenant WILLIAM P. HALL, Quartermaster.

First Lieutenant WALTER S. SCHUYLER, A.D.C. to General Crook.

Second Lieutenant CHARLES D. PARKHURST.

Second Lieutenant CHARLES H. WATTS (until July, when disabled).

Second Lieutenant EDWARD W. KEYES.

Second Lieutenant ROBERT LONDON.

Second Lieutenant GEORGE O. EATON (until August 24th, disabled August 10th).

Second Lieutenant HOEL S. BISHOP.

Lieutenant WM. C. HUNTER, U.S.N. ("Brevet Commodore").

Second Lieutenant ROBT. H. YOUNG, 4th Inf., A.D.C. to General Merritt.

Second Lieutenant J. HAYDEN PARDEE, 23d Inf., A.D.C. to General Merritt.

Second Lieutenant SATTERLEE C. PLUMMER, 4th Inf., with Co. "I."

Acting Assistant Surgeon J. W. POWELL.